THE GLASS MENAGERIE

Other titles in the Greenhaven Press Literary Companion Series:

American Authors

Maya Angelou
Stephen Crane
Emily Dickinson
William Faulkner
F. Scott Fitzgerald
Nathaniel Hawthorne
Ernest Hemingway
Herman Melville
Arthur Miller
Eugene O'Neill
Edgar Allan Poe
John Steinbeck
Mark Twain
Thornton Wilder

British Authors

Jane Austen
Joseph Conrad
Charles Dickens

World Authors

Fyodor Dostoyevsky
Homer
Sophocles

American Literature

The Adventures of
   Huckleberry Finn
The Catcher in the Rye
The Great Gatsby
Of Mice and Men
The Scarlet Letter

British Literature

Animal Farm
Beowulf
The Canterbury Tales
Lord of the Flies
Romeo and Juliet
Shakespeare: The Comedies
Shakespeare: The Histories
Shakespeare: The Sonnets
Shakespeare: The Tragedies
A Tale of Two Cities

World Literature

The Diary of a Young Girl

THE GREENHAVEN PRESS
Literary Companion
TO AMERICAN LITERATURE

READINGS ON

THE GLASS MENAGERIE

David Bender, *Publisher*
Bruno Leone, *Executive Editor*
Brenda Stalcup, *Managing Editor*
Bonnie Szumski, *Series Editor*
Thomas Siebold, *Book Editor*

Greenhaven Press, San Diego, CA

Every effort has been made to trace the owners of copy-righted material. The articles in this volume may have been edited for content, length, and/or reading level. The titles have been changed to enhance the editorial purpose of the Opposing Viewpoints® concept. Those interested in locating the original source will find the complete citation on the first page of each article.

Library of Congress Cataloging-in-Publication Data

Readings on The glass menagerie / Thomas Siebold, book
    editor.
        p.   cm. — (The Greenhaven Press literary
    companion to American literature)
    Includes bibliographical references and index.
    ISBN 1-56510-829-9 (lib. : alk. paper). —
ISBN 1-56510-828-0 (pbk. : alk. paper)
    1. Williams, Tennessee, 1911–1983. Glass menagerie.
I. Siebold, Thomas. II. Series.
PS3545.I5365G539   1998
812'.54—dc21   97-41140
                                                          CIP

Cover photo: Photofest

Copyright ©1998 by Greenhaven Press, Inc.
PO Box 289009
San Diego, CA 92198-9009
Printed in the U.S.A.

"High station in life is earned by the gallantry with which appalling experiences are survived with grace."

—Tennessee Williams, *Memoirs*

Contents

Chapter 1: Overview of Tennessee Williams and His Work

1. Williams's Struggle with Success
by Tennessee Williams   30

Williams's sudden rise to fame after the production of *The Glass Menagerie* left him with a sense of spiritual dislocation. He realized that he needed to stay involved in life's everyday struggles to maintain his sense of compassion and moral conviction.

2. Williams's Aristocratic Heroine
by Robert Emmet Jones   36

The aristocratic heroines of Williams's early plays attempt to recapture the gentility of the Old South, but they can't because that world has failed and given way to a modern society. As a result, these heroines lead pathetic, self-deluded lives victimized by their defeated pride, their illusions, and their failure to face reality.

Chapter 2: Themes and Characterization in *The Glass Menagerie*

1. The Episodic Structure of *The Glass Menagerie*
by Felicia Hardison Londré   46

In its broadest terms *The Glass Menagerie* is a dramatic poem about human nature. The play consists of seven tightly composed scenes that flow from Tom's memory.

2. Illusion Versus Reality in *The Glass Menagerie*
by Nilda G. Joven   52

A central theme in *The Glass Menagerie* is the conflict between illusion and reality. Williams presents the illusions of the Wingfield family as both vulnerable to the harshness of reality and beautiful, poetic, and charming.

Chapter 3: Structure, Influences, and Criticism of *The Glass Menagerie*

Foreword

"'Tis the good reader that
makes the good book."

Ralph Waldo Emerson

The story's bare facts are simple: The captain, an old and scarred seafarer, walks with a peg leg made of whale ivory. He relentlessly drives his crew to hunt the world's oceans for the great white whale that crippled him. After a long search, the ship encounters the whale and a fierce battle ensues. Finally the captain drives his harpoon into the whale, but the harpoon line catches the captain about the neck and drags him to his death.

A simple story, a straightforward plot—yet, since the 1851 publication of Herman Melville's *Moby-Dick*, readers and critics have found many meanings in the struggle between Captain Ahab and the whale. To some, the novel is a cautionary tale that depicts how Ahab's obsession with revenge leads to his insanity and death. Others believe that the whale represents the unknowable secrets of the universe and that Ahab is a tragic hero who dares to challenge fate by attempting to discover this knowledge. Perhaps Melville intended Ahab as a criticism of Americans' tendency to become involved in well-intentioned but irrational causes. Or did Melville model Ahab after himself, letting his fictional character express his anger at what he perceived as a cruel and distant god?

Although literary critics disagree over the meaning of *Moby-Dick*, readers do not need to choose one particular interpretation in order to gain an understanding of Melville's novel. Instead, by examining various analyses, they can gain numerous insights into the issues that lie under the surface of the basic plot. Studying the writings of literary critics can also aid readers in making their own assessments of *Moby-Dick* and other literary works and in developing analytical thinking skills.

The Greenhaven Literary Companion Series was created with these goals in mind. Designed for young adults, this unique anthology series provides an engaging and comprehensive introduction to literary analysis and criticism. The essays included in the Literary Companion Series are chosen for their accessibility to a young adult audience and are expertly edited in consideration of both the reading and comprehension levels of this audience. In addition, each essay is introduced by a concise summation that presents the contributing writer's main themes and insights. Every anthology in the Literary Companion Series contains a varied selection of critical essays that cover a wide time span and express diverse views. Wherever possible, primary sources are represented through excerpts from authors' notebooks, letters, and journals and through contemporary criticism.

Each title in the Literary Companion Series pays careful consideration to the historical context of the particular author or literary work. In-depth biographies and detailed chronologies reveal important aspects of authors' lives and emphasize the historical events and social milieu that influenced their writings. To facilitate further research, every anthology includes primary and secondary source bibliographies of articles and/or books selected for their suitability for young adults. These engaging features make the Greenhaven Literary Companion Series ideal for introducing students to literary analysis in the classroom or as a library resource for young adults researching the world's great authors and literature.

Exceptional in its focus on young adults, the Greenhaven Literary Companion Series strives to present literary criticism in a compelling and accessible format. Every title in the series is intended to spark readers' interest in leading American and world authors, to help them broaden their understanding of literature, and to encourage them to formulate their own analyses of the literary works that they read. It is the editors' hope that young adult readers will find these anthologies to be true companions in their study of literature.

INTRODUCTION

Readings on The Glass Menagerie is designed to help students gain a greater appreciation of one of Tennessee Williams's most significant plays. The carefully edited articles provide an overview of the play's themes, characterization, structure, philosophy, and impact on American theater. Each of the essays is readable, manageable in length, and focuses on concepts suitable for a beginning exploration into the genre of literary criticism. Additionally, this diverse overview of *The Glass Menagerie* presents students with a wealth of material for writing reports, designing oral presentations, or enriching their understanding of drama as art.

A study of *The Glass Menagerie* is an important component in a student's understanding of America's theatrical and literary history. With this play, Williams broke from the conventional realism that had, at the time, dominated the American stage. The play's subtle characterization, poetic language, creative use of lighting and music, and nostalgic mood work to portray subjective, inner emotions rather than objective reality. From its first staging at the Civic Theater in Chicago in 1944, *The Glass Menagerie* was destined to place Tennessee Williams at the forefront of modern American drama.

The critical essays in *Readings on* The Glass Menagerie will also help students to comprehend the meaning of the play, discover new methods of evaluating it, and appreciate the structure of its dramatic form. By reading the interpretations of literary critics, students will develop a meaningful vocabulary for approaching fundamental literary questions about the playwright's themes, characters, philosophy, and language.

In addition to the essays, *Readings on* The Glass Menagerie provides other pertinent material about Tennessee Williams. A biographical sketch offers readers background into the author's life and artistic influence. The chronology provides a useful overview of Williams's works and places them in a historical context. The bibliography identifies valuable resources for students performing further research.

With the production of *The Glass Menagerie*, Williams was lifted out of obscurity and placed in the strata of America's theatrical elite. The lyrical power of the play unfalteringly lingers in the minds of audiences. There is something disturbing yet appealing, even poetic, about witnessing the dissolution of sensitive, yet doomed, characters. The Wingfield family is broken; mother, son, and daughter are fragmented and unprepared to cope with an overwhelming and deterministic world. *The Glass Menagerie* is a startling and moving glimpse of the human condition; *Readings on* The Glass Menagerie organizes an enjoyable, provocative, and critical look at one of America's most touching plays.

TENNESSEE WILLIAMS: A BIOGRAPHY

Six years before he gained fame and wealth with *The Glass Menagerie*, Thomas Lanier Williams III published the short story "The Field of Blue Children" under the pen name Tennessee. He once stated that his given name "is a nice enough name, perhaps a little too nice. It sounds like it might belong to the sort of writer who turns out sonnet sequences to Spring." Tennessee was not only a nod to paternal ancestors who were Indian fighters in Tennessee, but also a vigorous-sounding name that fit his sense of who he was. It symbolized his restless and adventurous spirit; throughout his life, Williams was a seeker who frequently gave in to wanderlust that carried him from New York to California and from Iowa to Florida. The name defined his resolve; Williams fought not only the many battles required of a young writer to be successful, but also personal demons that drove him to several nervous breakdowns, drug addiction, and a nagging hypochondria. Tennessee strove to write symbolic and lyrical works that peeled away comfortable illusions and presented the audience with a searching exploration of life's realities.

THE WILLIAMS FAMILY

The playwright was born on March 26, 1911, in Columbus, Mississippi, deep in the heart of the American South. He was the second of three children born to Cornelius Coffin "C.C." Williams and Edwina Dakin "Miss Edwina" Williams. Daughter Rose Isabel was two years older than Thomas, and the playwright's younger brother, Walter Dakin, was born in 1919. Cornelius Williams's lineage had been a notable one, including the first chancellor of the Western Territory, Thomas Lanier Williams, and Tennessee's first senator, John Williams. Unfortunately, Tennessee Williams's paternal grandfather, Thomas Lanier Williams II, recklessly

13

squandered the family fortune running misguided and unsuccessful campaigns for the governorship of Tennessee, ultimately eroding the family's prominence and forcing the sale of the imposing family residence in Knoxville, which was turned into an orphanage.

C.C. Williams was a brusque, aggressive, and humorless person who as a young man studied law for two years at the University of Tennessee and served as a second lieutenant during the Spanish-American War. After a few short-term jobs, C.C. became a successful traveling salesman for the International Shoe Company, a profession that suited him. His work as a drummer kept him on the road and away from his family, a way of life that did not seem to bother him. He was a very heavy drinker and, according to Williams, "he acquired a great taste for poker and for light ladies—which was another source of distress to my mother." In his youth, Tom hated his father, who was very hard and distant toward his children, but many years later, after much psychoanalysis, the playwright recognized two important virtues in his father: "total honesty and total truth, as he saw it, in his dealings with others."

Williams's mother, Miss Edwina, was a beautiful southern belle whose upbringing was religious and proper, even puritanical. Her father, the Reverend Walter E. Dakin, was an Episcopal clergyman and her mother, Rose (Grand) Dakin, taught piano and violin. Miss Edwina's family had a history of mental and nervous disorders and she herself was often on the verge of hysteria which, later in her life, worsened and led to her commitment to a psychiatric ward. As a mother, she was overly protective. In his memoirs Williams wrote that "Miss Edwina never seemed to want me to have any friends. The boys were too rough for her delicate son, Tom, and the girls were, of course, too 'common.'"

CHILDHOOD

For the first eight years of Tom's life, the family lived with his maternal grandparents in the Columbus Episcopal rectory. In Cornelius's absence, the grandfather taught the strict religious values of an old South that was rapidly giving way to a more modern world with different values. For Williams, this was an innocent, even idyllic time in which he and his devoted sister, Rose, played games of the imagination with their black nurse, Ozzie, who told them fanciful stories. Only on occasion would their father return home from the road to intrude upon the gracious and closed world that Tom and his sister had created. But this charmed time ended abruptly when Tom contracted diphtheria, which left him with partial paralysis of his legs for over two years and forced him to stay home from school, bedridden. His mother hovered over him during his illness, smothering him with motherly care. When he finally recovered his health, Williams had retreated into a debilitating shyness and effeminacy. The playwright wrote that "during this period of illness and solitary games, my mother's overly solicitous attention planted in me the makings of a sissy, much to my father's discontent. I was becoming a decided hybrid, different from the family line of frontiersmen-heroes of east Tennessee."

In 1919 the family moved to St. Louis when C.C. Williams accepted a management job there with a branch of the International Shoe Company. Their first house was on a pleasant residential street, but soon they moved into a rather shabby apartment. In fact, over a span of ten years in St. Louis they lived in sixteen different places, moving for reasons unknown to the young Williams. C.C.'s promotion meant that he was off the road and stuck in an office, where he was very unhappy and depressed. His drinking increased to the point that he eventually required treatment for alcoholism. Tom's poor health and his inability to play sports with the other boys at school made him a frequent target of boyish taunts. This isolation, coupled with their unstable living arrangements, led Tom and his sister to find solace in each other's company, and they grew very close. Often they would retreat into Rose's bedroom to play imaginative games with Rose's collection of glass animals. Reflecting back on this period, Williams stated that the animals represented for him "all the softest emotions that belong to recollections of things past. They stood for all the tender things that relieve the austere pattern of life and make it endurable to the sensitive." Tom's only other friend was a neighborhood girl named Hazel Kramer who met Tom when he was eleven and she was nine. Hazel became Tom's closest childhood friend, and, later, a serious romantic interest. It was at this time also that he began to write stories, perhaps to counter his feelings of loneliness.

Tom attended University City High School in St. Louis, where he was an average student; English was his best subject and mathematics his worst. He was traumatized in adolescence by an extreme, almost pathological shyness, rendering him virtually incapable of speaking aloud in the classroom. Williams wrote that "it was at University City High School that I developed the habit of blushing whenever anyone looked me in the eyes, as if I harbored behind them some quite dreadful or abominable secret." Williams's explanation for this condition rested on his belief that another being was imprisoned deep within himself, a hidden schoolgirl, who blushed and trembled with a passing glance. Even Hazel, whom Tom loved and depended upon emotionally, made him blush.

Williams found partial relief from his shyness in two ways. Like Tom in *The Glass Menagerie,* Williams escaped to the movies. By his own admission, he was addicted to films as well as to movie magazines, which he bought by the armload even as an adult. His second means of escape was through writing. Using a typewriter that his mother gave him, Williams wrote and won a third-place prize for a letter answering the question "Can a good wife be a good sport?" The letter became his first published work when it appeared in the May 1927 issue of *Smart Set* magazine. One of Williams's short stories, "The Vengeance of Nitocris," a horror story, was published in the August 1928 *Weird Tales;* he received thirty-five dollars for his effort. In 1929 Williams graduated fifty-third in his class of eighty-three at University City High School.

In his memoirs Williams elaborates on an incident during his adolescence that he calls "the most nearly psychotic crisis that occurred in my early life." In 1928 Grandfather Dakin took his sixteen-year-old grandson on a church tour of Europe. While Williams was walking alone down a boulevard in Paris, he was struck with an overwhelming fear that, by his own account, pushed him "within a hairsbreadth of going quite mad." He had suddenly developed a phobia about the process of thinking, of thought itself. The incapacitating fear grew and grew throughout the remainder of the trip until Williams entered the Gothic cathedral in Cologne to pray. There he experienced "a miracle of a religious nature. It was as if an impalpable hand were placed upon my head, and at the instant of that touch, the phobia was lifted away as lightly as a snowflake though it had weighed on my head like a skull-breaking block of iron." Williams believed that the hand of Jesus had touched him to save him from madness. Although his plays are full of Christian symbols, particularly those portraying the image of Christ, Williams admitted as an adult that he never believed in the idea of life after death.

COLLEGE YEARS

In the autumn of 1929 Tom entered the University of Missouri at Columbia as a journalism major. His college career got off to a good start: he earned good grades, made the honor roll, joined a fraternity (Alpha Tau Omega), and competed on the school wrestling team in the 118-pound class. He also won a few prizes for his poetry as well as honorable mention in a drama contest for his one-act plays *Beauty Is the Word* and *Hot Milk at Three in the Morning*. However, two things happened to sour his college experience. First, Hazel Kramer, with whom Tom was still deeply infatuated, wanted to join him at the University of Missouri, but the idea irritated Cornelius Williams, who disapproved of the relationship and committed himself to aborting the plans. He approached Hazel's grandfather, who worked in the sales department under Cornelius, the sales manager, and threatened to withdraw Tom if Hazel moved ahead with her plans. Defeated, Hazel enrolled at the University of Wisconsin. Then, upset by Hazel's departure, Tom failed a required reserve officer training corps program (ROTC), which offended his father's pride in the prestigious military tradition of the Williams family.

In 1933 Cornelius withdrew Tom and pushed him into a sixty-five-dollar-a-month position at the International Shoe Company. For three years, from 1933 to 1935, Tom did menial work at his father's company, a job that Williams said was "designed for insanity, it was a living death." To cope with the situation, he began writing every night and spending weekends at the library, where he read voraciously. But the strain became too much; the hated job, the late-night writing, a poor diet, the shocking news that Hazel had suddenly married someone else, and the early signs that his sister, Rose, was experiencing mental disorders caused a collapse requiring Tom's hospitalization for a nervous breakdown. On doctors' orders, he quit his job and moved to Memphis to recuperate in his grandfather's home. During his convalescence Tom collaborated with a neighbor, Bernice Dorothy Shapiro, on a play for a little theater group called the Garden Players. The one-act comedy, *Cairo! Shanghai! Bombay!,* met with modest success, to the delight of the young writer. Seeing something that he had written acted out onstage was a powerful stimulant: "On the program I was identified as the collaborator and was given second billing to Dorothy. Still, the laughter, genuine and loud, at the comedy I had written enchanted me."

By 1936 Tom was well enough to return to St. Louis, where he announced to his father that he wanted to be a writer; Cornelius renounced him. But with his mother's help, Tom returned to college at Washington University in St. Louis. It was there that Tom, despite his ongoing shyness, fraternized with a group of writers and poets led by Clark Mills McBurney. Inspired by McBurney and his "literary factory," Tom wrote a one-act play entitled *The Magic Tower,* which won first prize in a drama contest sponsored by a local theater guild. Encouraged and now more determined than ever to be a full-time writer, Tom made contact with a St. Louis theater group, the Mummers. This odd and eclectic collection of actors was organized by the dynamic and bohemian director Willard Holland, who not only encouraged Williams to write plays but staged Tom's short antiwar work, *Headlines.* In 1937 the Mummers produced Williams's first two full-length plays, *The Fugitive Kind* and *Candles to the Sun.* After the production of *The Fugitive Kind,* Williams reported that he got his "first taste of blood drawn by critics." After the closing of the play, at a rather drunken party at a cast member's downtown hotel room, a depressed Williams made a mad dash to throw himself out of the window, only to be tackled and restrained by friends.

Distracted, Tom's grades at Washington University dropped and he was forced to leave without a degree. With financial backing from his grandmother, Tom enrolled at the University of Iowa in Iowa City, enticed there by its fine writing program. While he was away at the University of Iowa, Rose, who had failed to hold a job or find the love that she desired, withdrew further and further into herself, finally suffering a complete breakdown and confinement in a mental hospital, diagnosed as schizophrenic with little hope for recovery. Cornelius and Miss Edwina, without alerting Tom, followed a doctor's recommendation and consented to submit Rose to an untested neurosurgical procedure called a prefrontal lobotomy. The operation worked to calm Rose but left her torpid and in need of institutionalization for the rest of her life. Although devastated by his sister's ordeal, Tom managed to earn a bachelor's degree in 1938 from the University of Iowa.

BOHEMIAN DAYS

At the age of twenty-seven, armed with his typewriter, phonograph, and a small collection of influential works, primarily the writings of Hart Crane, Tom Williams moved away from his family and settled in the French Quarter of New Orleans. Here he led the bohemian life of a young, struggling writer, supporting himself by working in restaurants. It was in New Orleans that Williams established his personality as a writer, learned to discipline his writing habits, and came in contact with a whole array of characters—sailors, prostitutes, artists, philosophers, and rebels—who helped him define his own search for meaning and freedom. It was in New Orleans also that Williams came to terms with his homosexuality, an issue that would find its way into many of his later plays.

Early in 1939 Williams entered a drama contest with three one-act plays collectively titled *American Blues.* On the entry form Williams first used the pen name Tennessee. He won not only first place but also a professional contract from literary agent Audrey Wood, who would become his personal manager for the next thirty years. With the encouragement of Wood, Williams, now officially Tennessee, published the short story "The Field of Blue Children" in the magazine *Story.* By the end of that summer, Tennessee Williams obtained a thousand-dollar Rockefeller grant to continue his writing.

Early in 1940 Tennessee went to New York City to attend a seminar in advanced playwriting with John Gassner at the New School for Social Research. Gassner was impressed with Williams's full-length play *Battle of Angels* and recommended it enthusiastically to the New York Theater Guild. Later that year, while traveling in Mexico and California, Williams read in a New York paper that *Battle of Angels* was to be part of the Theater Guild's 1940 season. With high hopes, Williams rushed to New York to attend rehearsals. The play was a colossal flop, however, and never made it past its trial run in Boston. Williams admitted that "the play was pretty far out for its time and included, among other tactical errors, a mixture of super religiosity and hysterical sexuality coexisting in a central character. The critics and police censors seemed to regard this play as a theatrical counterpart of the bubonic plague surfacing in their city."

THE WAR YEARS

The years of World War II marked a low period for the aspiring playwright. Unable to serve in the military because of a weak heart, Williams drifted, holding various low-wage jobs in Provincetown, Macon, New York, Jacksonville, and St. Louis. Perhaps due to an accidental childhood injury, Williams developed a severe cataract in his left eye which required four separate operations. The ailing, discouraged writer moved to Key West to rewrite *Battle of Angels.*

In the spring of 1943, Audrey Wood called with good news: She had negotiated a position for Tennessee with Metro-Goldwyn-Mayer as a scenarist at a remarkable salary of $250 a week. Hopeful that this would be the break he was looking for, the thirty-two-year-old Williams moved to California to work at the studios. His first assignment was to adapt a script for Lana Turner for the film *Marriage Is a Private Affair.* MGM rejected his dialogue as unsuited to Miss Turner's style. Williams spitefully wrote in his memoirs that the actress "couldn't act her way out of her form-fitting cashmere but was an intimate friend of the producer who had engaged me and I was soon told that my dialogue was beyond the young lady's comprehension although I had avoided any language that was at all eclectic or multisyllabic." He then submitted an original script about a southern belle, but it too was rejected with the nasty comment that *Gone with the Wind* had already been done. Frustrated, Williams quit, only to discover that his contract guaranteed his salary for another four months. Elated, Williams rented a two-room apartment in Santa Monica and rewrote his southern belle film script into a stage play. The reworked material, based loosely on his own experience, became the three-act play entitled *The Glass Menagerie.*

SUCCESS AT LAST

Williams sent a copy of *The Glass Menagerie* to Audrey Wood with a note supposing that this play would be no more commercially successful than his previous work. Audrey disagreed; in fact, she loved the script, recognizing in it something extraordinary. She promptly sent it to actor-director-producer Eddie Dowling, who was deeply moved by the lyrical, nostalgic aspect of the work. He agreed to direct it and convinced the actress Laurette Taylor to come out of semi-retirement to play Amanda; he saved the role of Tom Wingfield for himself.

The play opened in Chicago on December 26, 1944. During rehearsals everyone, including Williams, thought that the play was doomed to failure since Laurette Taylor did not seem to know her lines or understand the depth of her character. The financial backer of the play, a mysterious character named Louis J. Singer, who owned a string of run-down hotels, attended a rehearsal and, according to Williams, "nearly died of apoplexy when he saw what he saw and heard what he did in that rehearsal hall." Minutes before the opening curtain, a missing Taylor was found in the bathroom dyeing a bathrobe she was scheduled to wear in the second act. When the curtain rose, however, Taylor and the rest of the cast gave a stunning performance that mesmerized the audience and the Chicago critics. When subsequent attendance was surprisingly poor, Dowling considered closing the play, but the Chicago critic Claudia Cassidy never gave up; almost daily she exhorted her readers to witness for themselves the remarkable dramatic experience by the new playwright Tennessee Williams. Looking back on the play's opening, Williams wrote in his memoirs that

> no one knew how to take *Menagerie;* it was something of an innovation in the theatre . . . even though Laurette gave an incredibly luminous, electrifying performance, and people observed it. But people are people, and most of them went home afterward to take at least equal pleasure in their usual entertainments. It took that lovely lady, Claudia Cassidy, the drama critic of the Chicago *Tribune,* a lot of time to sell it to them, to tell them it was special.

Suddenly *The Glass Menagerie* was a startling success, with a full house every night. When the play opened at the Playhouse Theater on Broadway on March 31, 1945, it received rave reviews and instantly became a huge commercial and artistic success. The play ran for 561 performances; in April 1945 the prestigious New York Drama Critics Circle named *The Glass Menagerie* best American play of the year. After a long struggle, Tennessee Williams, at the age of thirty-four, was established as a major voice in American theater.

A PERIOD OF PRODUCTIVITY

Williams's new status and popularity interfered with the completion of two plays that he was working on in 1946, *Poker Night*, later renamed *A Streetcar Named Desire*, and *Summer and Smoke*. Hence, in the spring of the year Williams rented a summer cottage on Nantucket Island to work and get away from the responsibilities and burden of success. While there, he suffered anxiety attacks brought on by his ongoing fear of heart failure. To help him cope with his nerves, Williams invited writer Carson McCullers, author of the 1939 novel *The Heart Is a Lonely Hunter*, to keep him company. Although they had previously only corresponded by mail, McCullers accepted and by the summer's end she had finished her play *A Member of the Wedding* and Williams had a draft of *Summer and Smoke*. The two became lifelong friends.

In the autumn of 1947 Williams obtained a little apartment in New Orleans, where he worked furiously to finish *A Streetcar Named Desire*. At the time, Williams was suffering from the hypochondriacal notion that he was dying of pancreatic cancer, generating a great urgency to finish the project. He wrote from early morning to midafternoon every day, and after a late lunch and several drinks he would go to the athletic club and swim; Williams was an avid swimmer throughout most of his life.

A Streetcar Named Desire opened on December 3, 1947, at the Barrymore Theater in New York. When the curtain fell, the audience applauded for over a half hour, the critics praised it unanimously, and Williams's artistry, introduced with *The Glass Menagerie*, was reaffirmed. The big hit of the cast was a young method actor named Marlon Brando, who played the virile Stanley Kowalski. The play ran for 855 performances and won the Donaldson Award, New York Drama Critics Circle Award, and the Pulitzer Prize. Additionally, the play began a productive association between Williams and Elia Kazan, the brilliant stage and film director who would go on to produce several more of Williams's plays as well as numerous film versions of his work. Williams admitted that at times he would write specifically for Kazan, stating that "what made him a great director was that he had an infinite understanding of people on an incredible level."

Before *A Streetcar Named Desire* closed on Broadway, the playwright received news that his mother and father had separated. Although time had helped to soften Williams's opinion of his father, he wrote that a divorce for Cornelius would "be a bitter end to a blind and selfish life."

After spending some time in Italy to relax and get away from family squabbles, the eastern press, and the rigors of fame, Williams, now with considerable wealth, bought a house in Key West, Florida. He lived there with his elderly grandfather and Frank Merlo, whom the playwright had met in Provincetown in 1948. Merlo and Williams would remain partners for over fourteen years; the playwright would dedicate *The Rose Tattoo* to Merlo, calling it his "love play to the world." This time in Williams's life marked the beginning of his most productive and successful period as an artist. Williams's plays were a regular feature on Broadway: *Summer and Smoke*, 1948; *The Rose Tattoo*, 1951, won the Tony Award for best play; *Camino Real*, 1953, received largely negative reviews; *Cat on a Hot Tin Roof*, 1955, won the New York Drama Critics Award and the Pulitzer Prize; *Orpheus Descending*, 1957, closed to bad reviews after only sixty-eight performances; *Sweet Bird of Youth*, 1959; and *The Night of the Iguana*, 1961, won the New York Drama Critics Award and the London Critics' Poll for best new foreign play. Williams's plays helped establish the reputations of some of the most notable American actors, including Marlon Brando, Jessica Tandy, Karl Malden, Burl Ives, Maureen Stapleton, Paul Newman, Eli Wallach, and Geraldine Page. Moreover, many of Williams's works were made into films, the rights for which earned him huge sums of money. *Sweet Bird of Youth*, for example, sold for an incredible $400,000 in 1959. By 1962, when Williams appeared on the cover of *Time* magazine, he was worth millions.

Despite his artistic and material success, Williams suffered an acute bout of depression in 1957, accompanied by claustrophobia, panic, and hypochondria. Several factors seemed to contribute to his troubled state of mind. In February 1955, Grandfather Dakin died at the age of ninety-seven. Williams had developed a deep love and admiration for his gentle grandfather, who had lived and traveled with him since 1948. In tribute to the gentleman, Williams spread a blanket of English violets, Dakin's favorite flower, over the gravesite. As *Orpheus Descending* was failing in 1957, the playwright received news that his father had died at the age of seventy-seven. Williams had not yet come to terms with his father's cruelties and his family's dysfunction. To make matters worse, he was relying more and more on alcohol and drugs, which he started using regularly in 1955. After his father's funeral, Williams entered intense psychoanalysis.

THE "STONED AGE"

The 1960s was a period of turmoil for Tennessee Williams. His life and career were disrupted by a general shift in society as a whole and by several personal tragedies. Public taste in the '60s shifted amid the war in Vietnam, the peace initiative, the civil rights struggle, and numerous liberation movements. Williams's style seemed dated; even his once daring themes of homosexuality seemed passé in light of the more militant gay rights movement. Audiences were turning to new playwrights like Edward Albee, Eugene Ionesco, and Samuel Beckett, who were working in a style called the theater of the absurd, avant-garde drama that reflects the illogical flow of events and the purposelessness of existence. Even the language of the absurdists challenged Williams's lyrical, poetical style by conveying meaning through sounds, nonsense dialogue, gestures, and stylized actions.

On a personal level, Williams suffered intense loss and agitation with the death of his companion, Frank Merlo, from cancer in 1963. In his memoirs he wrote that "it is difficult to write about a period of profound, virtually clinical depression, because when you are in that state, everything is observed through a dark glass which not only shadows but distorts all that is seen."

The playwright hoped to numb his sense of loss and loneliness with a combination of pills and alcohol, using both in such quantities that he wondered later if he was perhaps enacting an unconscious suicide attempt. Looking back on the decade, the playwright refers to the time as his "stoned age," a period that suggested "a slow-motion photo of a building being demolished by dynamite: it occurred in protracted stages, but the protraction gave it no comfort." At the nadir of his depression, he returned to New Orleans in a last solitary effort to pull himself together. By the time he got there he was almost reduced to mutism, unable to communicate much beyond grunts and odd sounds. He withdrew further and further, sustaining himself on one sauceless meal of spaghetti each day. After a disastrous treatment by a doctor that Williams mockingly called Dr. Feel Good because of the injections that he prescribed, Dakin, Williams's brother, thinking that Tennessee was going to die, convinced the playwright to convert to Catholicism. By the end of 1969 Williams experienced a severe nervous breakdown and was ultimately placed in a psychiatric ward in St. Louis.

His stay in the hospital was rough; he remembered the experience in an interview with his friend Dotson Rader: "They suddenly snatched away every pill I had! The injections went too. So I blacked out. It was cold turkey, baby. They tell me I had three brain convulsions in the course of one long day, and a coronary. How I survived, I don't know. I think there were homicidal intentions at work there." Despite his suffering and delirium, he was temporarily withdrawn from his dependency on drugs and liquor.

The plays during the "stoned age" were not well received. *Milk Train*, 1963, earned mixed reviews, mostly poor; *Slapstick Tragedy*, a 1966 double bill of two short plays, was shut down after just one week; and *In the Bar of a Tokyo Hotel* had a brief run of only twenty-five performances. Williams's remembrance of this period, although limited and vague, focused on the viciousness of the press, which he said "hit me with all the ammo in their considerable and rather ruthless possession."

THE FRUSTRATION OF THE 1970S AND 1980S

The 1970s and early 1980s were a time of frustration for Williams, as he searched to regain the critical esteem he enjoyed at the height of his career. In 1971 his play *Out Cry* was staged at the Ivanhoe Theater in Chicago. The play is an adventurous exploration of the playwright's relationship with his sister, Rose. The audience reception was cool. Williams's frustration with his lack of dramatic success over the previous decade seemed to come to a boiling point when he exploded at his longtime agent and manager Audrey Wood. He shouted at her, "You must have been pleased by the audience reaction tonight. You've wanted me dead for ten years. But I'm not going to die." Audrey stared at her client and friend with a dignified, calm look, said nothing, flew back to New York that night, and never served as his representative again. In his memoirs, the playwright tried to rationalize his behavior: "Perhaps if my feelings for her had been limited to professional ones, I would not have been so disturbed and finally so outraged when her concern for me appeared to ebb, so that I found myself alone as a child lost or an old dog abandoned."

After the lackluster run of *Out Cry*, Williams's next play, *Small Craft Warnings*, gave him his only commercial success since *The Night of the Iguana* in 1961. What makes *Small Craft Warning* unique is the fact that Williams made his professional acting debut in it as Doc, an alcoholic doctor who has lost his license. He decided to take the role in order to draw people into the play. In *Memoirs* Williams admits to making a few fluffs and lapsing into a few ad libs that disturbed his fellow actors, but all in all he played the role convincingly, got a big hand, and the play lasted for 192 off-Broadway performances.

The original title for *Small Craft Warning* was *Confessionals*, a heading that might apply to the autobiographical trend Williams was expressing in his last plays: *Vieux Carré*, 1977; *Something Cloudy, Something Clear*, 1981; and *A House Not Meant to Stand*, 1982. All clearly explore aspects of the writer's life. The two most revealing works, however, are not plays. *Moise and the World of Reason* is a semiautobiographical novel that explicitly explores homosexuality and *Memoirs* is an autobiography styled as a chatty, self-absorbed confession that makes the reader feel that he is secretly overhearing a revealing conversation between the author and his analyst.

After the humiliation of *Out Cry*, Williams resumed a heavy use of drugs and alcohol, resulting in bouts of disorientation, anxiety, and loneliness. In 1980 he received the awaited news that his mother, Miss Edwina, had died at the age of ninety-five. At the funeral in St. Louis the playwright was reunited with his brother, Dakin. Tennessee had been estranged from his brother, blaming him for cruelly committing him to a psychiatric ward in 1969 and for attempting to appropriate a large percentage of *The Glass Menagerie*'s royalties, which continued through the years to be very valuable. The brothers reconciled, Dakin was reinstated in Tennessee's will, and the two traveled together with Rose to the White House where President Jimmy Carter presented Tennessee the Presidential Medal of Freedom, the highest civilian award given by the government. Williams was deeply moved by Carter's presentation statement, which read, "Tennessee Williams has shaped the history of American drama. From passionate tragedy to lyrical comedy, his masterpieces dramatize the eternal conflict of body and soul, youth and death, love and despair. Through the unity of reality and poetry Tennessee Williams shows that the truly heroic in life or art is human compassion."

Williams once said that he would continue to write even on his deathbed. And in truth he was still working on a play called *Masks Outrageous* when he choked to death in his modest room at the Elysee Hotel in New York in 1983. The autopsy showed that the playwright had been taking barbiturates and choked on a plastic medicine cap, the kind used on eyedrops or nasal spray bottles. A man preoccupied with his own death, Williams wrote in *Memoirs,* "I hope to die in my sleep, when the time comes, and I hope it will be in the beautiful big brass bed in my New Orleans apartment." Upon hearing of his brother's death, Dakin stated that he was not surprised because he had known for three months that Tennessee's health was deteriorating rapidly. Williams is buried between the graves of his mother and his sister.

CONCLUSION

Tennessee Williams's journey as a writer was a convoluted mix of distinct ups and downs: his formative years marked by extreme shyness and sexual confusion; the breakthrough years with the glory and success of *The Glass Menagerie*; his recognition as one of America's great writers during the '50s; his "stoned age," when he succumbed to drugs, alcohol, and depression; his time in recovery after a stay in a psychiatric hospital; and his years of frustration attempting to regain the power of his writing. In 1981, two years before his death, Williams wrote:

> I now look back at periods of my life, and I think, Was that really me? Was I doing those things? I don't feel any continuity in my life. It is as if my life were segments that are separate and do not connect. From one period to another it has all happened behind the curtain of work. And I just peek out from behind the curtain now and then and find myself on totally different terrain.

Tennessee Williams wrote plays for over thirty years, experiencing both the rewards and the humiliations of being a writer. He started writing when he was twelve, and by the time he was in his teens he wrote every day, regularly pumping himself up with black coffee and cigarettes so he could stay awake nearly all night working. Finally, at age thirty-four and nearly at the end of his stamina, he roared into money and fame with *The Glass Menagerie*. When his works connected with audiences the results were spectacular, but when they failed, as many did, he suffered a painful sense of rejection and loneliness. Williams claimed that he was born a writer, that he had to write, not for an audience but mainly for himself, almost as therapy to expose and deal with inner turmoil and doubts. He often stated that his semi-autobiographical plays grew from within, sweeping over him like apparitions that materialized from the psychological currents of his life.

Frequently Tennessee Williams tested the patience of his friends and family: He was a hypochondriac, he was restless, he often said hurtful things to those closest to him, he was chemically dependent, he suffered with raw nerves, his sexual frankness bordered at times on exhibitionism, he was afraid of success, he had an inordinate fear of insanity, and he was obsessed with his own death. But as an artist he was a fighter, seemingly imbued with the ruggedness that his forefathers exhibited in the Tennessee frontier. When discussing the reasons for his pen name, Tennessee claimed that writing was like defending a frontier stockade against hostile invaders.

In the *New York Post*, American playwright Arthur Miller, a contemporary of Williams's, reacted to Tennessee's death and career with this assessment:

> He came into the theatre bringing his poetry, his hardened edge of romantic adoration of the lost and the beautiful. For a while, the theatre loved him, and then it went back to searching in its pockets for its soul. He chose a hard life that requires the skin of an alligator and the heart of a poet. To his everlasting honor, he persevered and bore all of us toward glory.

CHAPTER 1

Overview of Tennessee Williams and His Work

Williams's Struggle with Success

Tennessee Williams

Williams's essay "The Catastrophe of Success" appeared first in the *New York Times* and later as the introduction to the New Classics edition of *The Glass Menagerie.* With the production of *The Glass Menagerie,* Williams experienced the American version of the Cinderella story: He was catapulted from obscurity to sudden prominence. Williams writes that fame and wealth brought on a "spiritual dislocation," marked by cynicism, isolation, and indifference to others. The playwright withdrew from the pressures of fame and his public self to a hospital confinement for an eye operation and, later, an extended stay in Mexico.

Williams argues that an individual needs a certain level of struggle in one's life in order to give it meaning. The storybook public life is a fiction full of false images. The artist must stay enmeshed in human affairs to nurture compassion, moral conviction, and purity of heart.

This winter marked the third anniversary of the Chicago opening of "The Glass Menagerie," an event that terminated one part of my life and began another about as different in all external circumstances as could well be imagined. I was snatched out of virtual oblivion and thrust into sudden prominence, and from the precarious tenancy of furnished rooms about the country I was removed to a suite in a first-class Manhattan hotel. My experience was not unique. Success has often come that abruptly into the lives of Americans. The Cinderella story is our favorite national myth, the cornerstone of the film industry if not of the Democracy itself. I have seen it enacted on the screen so often that I was now inclined to yawn at it, not with disbelief but with an attitude of Who Cares! Anyone with such beautiful teeth and hair as the screen protagonist of such a story was bound to have a good time one way or another, and you could bet your bottom dollar and all the tea in China that that one would not be caught dead or alive at any meeting involving a social conscience.

No, my experience was not exceptional, but neither was it quite ordinary, and if you are willing to accept the somewhat eclectic proposition that I had not been writing with such an experience in mind—and many people are not willing to believe that a playwright is interested in anything but popular success—there may be some point in comparing the two estates.

WILLIAMS'S CLIMB TO FAME

The sort of life that I had had previous to this popular success was one that required endurance, a life of clawing and scratching along a sheer surface and holding on tight with raw fingers to every inch of rock higher than the one caught hold of before, but it was a good life because it was the sort of life for which the human organism is created.

I was not aware of how much vital energy had gone into this struggle until the struggle was removed. I was out on a level plateau with my arms still thrashing and my lungs still grabbing at air that no longer resisted. This was security at last.

I sat down and looked about me and was suddenly very depressed. I thought to myself, this is just a period of adjustment. Tomorrow morning I will wake up in this first-class hotel suite above the discreet hum of an East Side boulevard and I will appreciate its elegance and luxuriate in its comforts and know that I have arrived at our American plan of Olympus. Tomorrow morning when I look at the green satin sofa I will fall in love with it. It is only temporarily that the green satin looks like slime on stagnant water.

But in the morning the inoffensive little sofa looked more revolting than the night before and I was already getting too fat for the $125 suit which a fashionable acquaintance had selected for me. In the suite things began to break accidentally. An arm came off the sofa. Cigarette burns appeared on the polished surface of the furniture. Windows were left upon and a rain storm flooded the suite. But the maid always put it straight and the patience of the management was inexhaustible. Late parties could not offend them seriously. Nothing short of a demolition bomb seemed to bother my neighbors.

I lived on room service. But in this, too, there was a disenchantment. Some time between the moment when I ordered dinner over the phone and when it was rolled into my living room like a corpse on a rubber-wheeled table, I lost all interest in it. Once I ordered a sirloin steak and a chocolate sundae, but everything was so cunningly disguised on the table that I mistook the chocolate sauce for gravy and poured it over the sirloin steak.

WILLIAMS'S SPIRITUAL DISLOCATION

Of course all this was the more trivial aspect of a spiritual dislocation that began to manifest itself in far more disturbing ways. I soon found myself becoming indifferent to people. A well of cynicism rose in me. Conversations all sounded as if they had been recorded years ago and were being played back on a turntable. Sincerity and kindliness seemed to have gone out of my friends' voices. I suspected them of hypocrisy. I stopped calling them, stopped seeing them. I was impatient of what I took to be inane flattery.

I got so sick of hearing people say, "I loved your play!" that I could not say thank you any more. I choked on the words and turned rudely away from the usually sincere person. I no longer felt any pride in the play itself but began to dislike it, probably because I felt too lifeless inside ever to create another. I was walking around dead in my shoes and I knew it but there were no friends I knew or trusted sufficiently, at that time, to take them aside and tell them what was the matter.

This curious condition persisted about three months, till late spring, when I decided to have another eye operation mainly because of the excuse it gave me to withdraw from the world behind a gauze mask. It was my fourth eye operation, and perhaps I should explain that I had been afflicted for about five years with a cataract on my left eye which required a series of needling operations and finally an operation on the muscle of the eye. (The eye is still in my head. So much for that.)

Well, the gauze mask served a purpose. While I was resting in the hospital the friends whom I had neglected or affronted in one way or another began to call on me and now that I was in pain and darkness, their voices seemed to have changed, or rather that unpleasant mutation which I had suspected earlier in the season had now disappeared and they sounded now as they had used to sound in the lamented days of my obscurity. Once more they were sincere and kindly voices with the ring of truth in them and that quality of understanding for which I had originally sought them out.

As far as my physical vision was concerned, this last operation was only relatively successful (although it left me with an apparently clear black pupil in the right position, or nearly so) but in another, figurative way, it had served a much deeper purpose.

When the gauze mask was removed I found myself in a readjusted world. I checked out of the handsome suite at the first-class hotel, packed my papers and a few incidental belongings and left for Mexico, an elemental country where you can quickly forget the false dignities and conceits imposed by success, a country where vagrants innocent as children curl up to sleep on the pavements and human voices, especially when their language is not familiar to the ear, are soft as birds'. My public self, that artifice of mirrors, did not exist here and so my natural being was resumed.

Then, as a final act of restoration, I settled for a while at Chapala to work on a play called "The Poker Night," which later became "A Streetcar Named Desire." It is only in his work that an artist can find reality and satisfaction, for the actual world is less intense than the world of his invention and consequently his life, without recourse to violent disorder, does not seem very substantial. The right condition for him is that in which his work is not only convenient but unavoidable.

For me a convenient place to work is a remote place among strangers where there is good swimming. But life should require a certain minimal effort. You should not have too many people waiting on you, you should have to do most things for yourself. Hotel service is embarrassing. Maids, waiters, bellhops, porters and so forth are the most embarrassing people in the world for they continually remind you of inequities which we accept as the proper thing. The sight of an ancient woman, gasping and wheezing as she drags a heavy pail of water down a hotel corridor to mop up the mess of some drunken overprivileged guest, is one that sickens and weighs upon the heart and withers it with shame for this world in which it is not only tolerated but regarded as proof positive that the wheels of Democracy are functioning as they should without interference from above or below. Nobody should have to clean up anybody else's mess in this world. It is terribly bad for both parties, but probably worse for the one receiving the service.

I have been corrupted as much as anyone else by the vast number of menial services which our society has grown to expect and depend on. We should do for ourselves or let the machines do for us, the glorious technology that is supposed to be the new light of the world. We are like a man who has bought a great amount of equipment for a camping trip, who has the canoe and the tent and the fishing lines and the axe and the guns, the mackinaw and the blankets, but who now, when all the preparations and the provisions are piled expertly together, is suddenly too timid to set out on the journey but remains where he was yesterday and the day before and the day before that, looking suspiciously through white lace curtains at the clear sky he distrusts. Our great technology is a God-given chance for adventure and for progress which we are afraid to attempt. Our ideas and our ideals remain exactly what they were and where they were three centuries ago. No. I beg your pardon. It is no longer safe for a man even to declare them!

THE VALUE OF CONFLICT AND STRUGGLE

This is a long excursion from a small theme into a large one which I did not intend to make, so let me go back to what I was saying before.

This is an oversimplification. One does not escape that easily from the seduction of an effete way of life. You cannot arbitrarily say to yourself, I will now continue my life as it was before this thing, Success, happened to me. But once you fully apprehend the vacuity of a life without struggle you are equipped with the basic means of salvation. Once you know this is true, that the heart of man, his body and his brain, are forged in a white-hot furnace for the purpose of conflict (the struggle of creation) and that with the conflict removed, the man is a sword cutting daisies, that not privation but luxury is the wolf at the door and that the fangs of this wolf are all the little vanities and conceits and laxities that Success is heir to—why, then with this knowledge you are at lease in a position of knowing where danger lies.

You know, then, that the public Somebody you are when you "have a name" is a fiction created with mirrors and that the only somebody worth being is the solitary and unseen you that existed from your first breath and which is the sum of your actions and so is constantly in a state of becoming under your own violation—and knowing these things, you can even survive the catastrophe of Success!

It is never altogether too late, unless you embrace the Bitch Goddess, as [American philosopher] William James called her, with both arms and find in her smothering caresses exactly what the homesick little boy in you always wanted, absolute protection and utter effortlessness. Security is a kind of death, I think, and it can come to you in a storm of royalty checks beside a kidney-shaped pool in Beverly Hills or anywhere at all that is removed from the conditions that made you an artist, if that's what you are or were or intended to be. Ask anyone who has experienced the kind of success I am talking about—What good is it? Perhaps to get an honest answer you will have to give him a shot of truth serum but the word he will finally groan is unprintable in genteel publications.

Then what is good? The obsessive interest in human affairs, plus a certain amount of compassion and moral conviction, that first made the experience of living something that must be translated into pigment or music or bodily movement or poetry or prose or anything that's dynamic and expressive—that's what's good for you if you're at all serious in your aims. [American short-story writer and novelist] William Saroyan wrote a great play on this theme, that purity of heart is the one success worth having. "In the time of your life—live!" That time is short and it doesn't return again. It is slipping away while I write this and while you read it, and the monosyllable of the clock is Loss, loss, loss, unless you devote your heart to its opposition.

Williams's Aristocratic Heroine

Robert Emmet Jones

Robert Emmet Jones suggests that the early plays of Tennessee Williams include two basic female types: women of the old aristocratic South who are unable to accept the modern world and women who are uncultured and sensual. Jones writes that the first type, aristocratic white heroines like Amanda Wingfield in *The Glass Menagerie*, are women who are haunted by the Old South, a world of lost dreams, failure, and fragile beauty. Their ties to the past prevent them from coping with the reality of the society in which they now live.

Jones argues that these women are caught in a double standard. Antebellum values place women on pure, virginal pedestals that required them to marry gentlemen, but these gentlemen have disappeared with the passing of the Old South. Hence, they face the dilemma of marrying below their assumed stations in life or becoming spinsters, a pathetic and demeaned status. The aristocratic heroines remain self-deluded, like social fossils, maintaining false aristocratic façades in which they verbally reject their sexuality, and deny it when they give in. According to Jones, these heroines are not tragic figures because they are defeated before the play even begins. They are too weak and neurotic to be tragic; the audience can pity them but cannot admire them. Jones believes the tragedy is in the culture that created them and ultimately cast them adrift in a modern world.

Robert Emmet Jones is a professor of French and humanities at Massachusetts Institute of Technology, Cambridge. His writings include *The Alienated Hero: Studies in the Contemporary French Drama* and *Gerard de Nerval*. He is also a contributor to *Modern Drama, French Review*, and *Kentucky Foreign Language Quarterly*.

From "Tennessee Williams, Early Heroines," by Robert Emmet Jones, *Modern Drama*, vol. 2 (December 1959), pp. 211–19. Reprinted by permission of *Modern Drama*.

Critics have generally agreed that the heroines of Tennessee Williams are his finest creations. They dominate the plays in which they are found, and to them, as representatives of certain Southern types, Williams has brought much insight. This insight, which is at once poetic and sociological, has, since 1945, provided the American theater with several characters who may well rank in future histories of American dramatic literature with Eugene O'Neill's Anna Christie and Nina Leeds as the most successful creations of dramatic heroines in the first half of the twentieth century.

TWO BASIC TYPES OF FEMALE CHARACTERS

There are basically two types of women in the plays of Williams: the women who are the relics of the moribund tradition of gentility in which Williams himself was reared, women who are unable to accept the twentieth century and who prefer living in the illusive and legendary world of something that never really was—the mythically cavalier Old South; and the healthy, uncultured, basically sensual women, usually of Latin origin, by whom Williams has been attracted in his more recent plays, and who seem to have been conceived by their creator, if not as representatives of a sort of salvation, then at least as attractive earth goddesses whose salvation is their own sexuality. I propose in this paper to study the first type of heroine, for by studying her, I believe, some important facets of the dramatic art of Tennessee Williams may be revealed.

The Civil War was as destructive to the Southern landlords as the French Revolution had been to the French nobility. Where once had been a rigid social system based on slavery and ruled by many cultured, wealthy aristocrats, there was, after the Civil War complete anarchy and loss of values. When the economic system on which this society had been based was destroyed, the society itself fell with it.

When his plantation was broken up, the Southern aristocrat was faced with three alternatives. He could accept the changes the war had made and conform to the new society. He could migrate west and start again, or he could retire from active life in the New South, live in a world of false values, and become increasingly alienated from the society which he had sired unknowingly and which had rejected him. The proudest (and the weakest, perhaps) chose the last way. It was certainly the easiest. But, as the years rolled

by, this group, still retaining its pre-war viewpoint and ig-
noring all who were not acceptable by the old standards,
steadily degenerated.

Tennessee Williams is the poet of this decline. His world
is the world of the New South with, in his early plays, espe-
cial emphasis on the place of the aristocrat in it. This world
is one of fragile beauty and unnatural horror, of lost dreams
and poetic visions, of animal sex and refined deviations, of
first-generation Americans and their blue-blooded wives, of
failure and unhappiness, seldom of success. It is a world of
yesterday and today, practically never of tomorrow. The
characters of Williams always look to the past for their salvation. They cannot understand the present or, if they do,
they are powerless to act within it because they will seldom
compromise with it. They are damned the moment they
come on stage.

WILLIAMS' ARISTOCRATIC HEROINE

It was during the years between 1944 and 1948, between the
writing of *Battle of Angels* and *A Streetcar Named Desire,* that
Williams created the character for which he is most
renowned—the neurotic Southern white woman of aristocratic origin. Be she Cassandra Whiteside of *Battle of Angels*
living among the poor white trash of a town in the deep
South, or Amanda Wingfield of *The Glass Menagerie* in the
slums of Saint Louis, or Blanche DuBois in a near-slum section of New Orleans, or Alma Winemiller of *Summer and
Smoke* in Glorious Hill, Mississippi, a sleepy town invaded
by the crass commercialism of the twentieth century, the
Williams heroine exists mainly in illusion, denying today
and living an imaginary yesterday. These women, of whom
Blanche and Amanda are the best realized, are haunted by
the past and cannot or will not cast off its fetters. They live
in a world of paper lanterns and moonlit lakes, a world of
gentility where courtly men crown them the eternal belle of
the ball, where everyone desires them and they save their fa-
vors for a phantom. They are pathetic because they are incapable of meeting and triumphing over the demands of
their times, and the society in which they live will not and
cannot accept them on their own terms.

These four women—Alma, Cassandra, Blanche, and
Amanda—have much in common and, in fact, are really the
same person at different stages of life. Alma Winemiller is in

the process of revolting against the limitations of her se-
cluded life as a minister's daughter in Glorious Hill.
Through an obvious metamorphosis, from a creature of re-
pression to one of sexual license, she becomes a willing
magnet to travelling salesmen. Cassandra Whiteside is the
same character who has been having nocturnal "gentlemen"
callers for many years. She is a decided nymphomaniac
whose main interests are men, liquor, and "jooking." She is
perverse and, unfortunately for her town and the few decent
people with whom she comes into contact, a law unto herself. Blanche DuBois has gone through the stages at which
we have seen Alma and Cassandra; through her sexual and
concomitant mental idiosyncracies, she has lost all contact
with reality and is ripe for a mental institution. Amanda had
married a telephone man who deserted her after siring their
two children. Only because she was domesticated at an early
age, Amanda does not become a nymphomaniac, but her
origins and her reactions to life indicate her absolute kinship
with Alma, Cassandra, and Blanche.

THE ARISTOCRATIC HEROINE'S DILEMMA

These aristocratic heroines of Tennessee Williams are, unfortunately, and this is their tragedy, the victims of a double
standard observed in the society in which they were reared.
To the Victorians—and the Old South in its later days was
predominantly Victorian—woman was the pure pedestaled
goddess worshipped from afar by the impure and animalistic
man whose saviour she was supposed to be. W.J. Cash says:

> the Yankee must be answered by proclaiming from the
> housetops that Southern Virtue, so far from being inferior,
> was superior, not alone to the North's but to any on earth, and
> adducing Southern Womanhood in proof.

> The upshot, in this land of spreading notions of chivalry, was
> downright gyneolatry.

Good women were supposedly sexless; they were not supposed to think about, much less enjoy the act of procreation.
Those who did were suspect, and female society, thus, con-
sisted of good women (sexless) and fallen women.

The men, as the society degenerated, sold their plantations piece by piece to finance their epic fornications, but the
ideal of the virginal woman remained the same, if it did not
actually become intensified. [Again, Cash:]

> Lastly, the increased centrality of woman, added up with the

fact that miscegenation, though more terrifying than it had been even in the Old South, showed little tendency to fall off despite efforts to build up standards against it, served to intensify the old interest in gyneolatry, and to produce yet more florid notions about Southern Womanhood and Southern Virtue, and so to foster yet more precious notions of modesty and decorous behaviour for the Southern female to live up to.

To the young ladies reared in the shadow of this antebellum standard, the twentieth century, whose modernizing influence was in many pernicious ways being felt in the South, was anathema. And yet it was impossible to live according to the old code. Formerly these girls would have been married by their families to wealthy planters and thus would have been assured of respectability within the social structure if they lived up to the standards set for them. However, the young planters and other eligible men had changed, too, as their society had evolved. No longer fettered by their own conventions, they married, usually for money, more full-blooded girls of the lower classes, the daughters of wealthy men who formerly had been socially unacceptable, and often for sexual reasons women their grandmothers would have ignored. Many of the planters were effete and impotent, often they were homosexual—like Blanche's husband, Allan. And, reared to be a lady, the girl who had no money and was terrified of becoming a spinster (the most pathetic and ill-treated being in the South) was faced with an impossible choice. Her pride forbade her marrying beneath her (although Blanche's sister, Stella, did just that) and demanded that she marry a gentleman even if he was sexually deficient. She would not and could not remain single. In *Battle of Angels* there are two women, Cassandra and Myra, who have already faced this choice, as had Amanda in *The Glass Menagerie,* and both *Summer and Smoke* and *A Streetcar Named Desire* are concerned with women who face the same problem.

Now since this choice is an impossible one, certain aspects of the characters of these various heroines influence their final actions and decisions. Due, no doubt, to the double standard mentioned before, each of these women is emotionally immature. Yet each, with the exception of the older Amanda, has strong sexual desires, usually tending towards nymphomania. Each began life in an atmosphere of refinement in a closed society where she tantalized, and rather sadistically so, the many gentlemen callers she received. Unconsciously she desired to belong to these men physically, but, because of the code under which she lived, she turned her desires into coquettishness, affectation, and evasion. She refused to admit the existence of sex as such; the thought of it was degrading. And the men who could find more profitable and less mentally exhausting sexual outlets elsewhere turned from her. With the realization that her youth was passing, this typical Williams heroine, giving way to her own desires, became desperate and eventually began to do whatever men wanted. Through giving her body she could at least belong, if she could not belong in any other way.

THE SEXUAL OBSESSION OF THE ARISTOCRATIC HEROINE

Sex obsesses her as it obsesses all Puritans. She is ever conscious of it. Notice, for example, the constant reactions of Alma, Blanche, and Cassandra to the male body. The physical side of life, which socially and verbally these heroines find so repulsive, exerts a mysterious and all-powerful fascination over them, and they finally submit to it and rationalize their reasons for doing so. Yet they are not wholly aware of what they are doing. Thus there is always something curiously virginal about them even though, technically, they are whores. Through sex, the great leveller of all society, however, they are degraded rather than exalted because they cannot give themselves over to it wholeheartedly. This is excellently indicated in *A Streetcar Named Desire* in a scene between Blanche and her sister, Stella. Stella has escaped the neuroticism to which her sister has fallen prey by completely accepting physical love with her husband, an animal-like Pole, Stanley Kowalski. Through her marriage she has become a Woman, much as Serafina of the later *The Rose Tattoo*. No matter how sordid her existence, no matter how degrading her compromise with life, Stella has security and a sense of fulfillment in her love for her husband. Blanche, who herself uses sex to cling to when all else is gone, cannot understand her sister's submission to what she believes is an animal-like existence.

> BLANCHE: Yes, you are, your fix is worse than mine is! Only you are not being sensible about it. I'm going to do something. Get hold of myself and make myself a new life!
> STELLA: Yes?
> BLANCHE: But you've given in. And that isn't right, you're not old! You can get out.
> STELLA: I'm not in anything I want to get out of.

The importance of the sexual function is extremely pervasive in the plays of Tennessee Williams, and it becomes a
liberating force in his later plays. In the earlier plays, however, it is a binding force because his heroines are ladies.
The heroines are always conscious of the fact that they are
ladies. They never forget it, nor will they allow others to do
so. Their heritage is something no one can ever take from
them, for they are all well-born; Blanche and Cassandra
come from the oldest families in their section of the country.
The early Williams heroine is, in her own mind, never anything but a lady, and a consciousness of the niceties of existence excuses her in her own eyes for her transgressions.
Blanche, amidst the squalor of her sister's home, still acts
the lady, and she really believes she is one, even though
Stanley attempts to break through her pride and convince
her she is just a common whore. Amanda, Blanche, and
Cassandra all remember the plantations on which they were
born, or where it must be assumed that they were born. Like
Alma in the rectory of her father, they were protected at
home by the social code. That this code has long since disappeared is obvious from the name of Blanche's family es-
tate—Belle Reve. The very name, with its grammatical in-
consistency, is a symbol of the degeneracy of the family and
of its flight from reality.

The fact that the changing social conditions of the world
have made it impossible for these heroines still to be protected by their past means that when these women are
thrown into the world they must accept it and adjust to it or
become outcasts from it. Cassandra will not adjust. She
prefers finding solace in liquor and men. Amanda lives completely in the past, as if the present did not exist, and her
family consequently goes to pieces. Alma cannot reconcile
her nascent sexuality with her puritanical rearing and becomes a neurasthenic and later a whore. Blanche is forced
to become a school teacher in order to preserve a shabby
gentility. Her search for something to which she may belong
finds roots only in casual affairs with men and boys. Eventually, because of her license, she is relieved of her teaching
duties and has to go to her sister for protection.

But these heroines never find anything in the contemporary world to replace their former security. Their past, or
rather their idealized past, cannot be recaptured. And yet
they seek to recapture it by various means. Blanche tries to

revive it through memory. She will not accept the fact that she must come to grips with reality and live according to its exigencies in order to retain some amount of sanity. She refuses reality:

> BLANCHE: I don't want realism.
> MITCH: Naw, I guess not.
> BLANCHE: I'll tell you what I want. Magic! *(Mitch laughs)* Yes, yes, magic! I try to give that to people. I misrepresent things to them. I don't tell the truth. I tell what ought to be the truth. And if that is sinful, then let me be damned for it!

To Blanche reality is an electric light bulb which is too blinding to be endured; everything must be seen by candlelight which never shows the shabbiness and horrors of the present. She says, "I can't stand a naked light bulb any more than I can a rude remark or vulgar action." If a light bulb is a symbol of reality in the plays of Tennessee Williams, there are many symbols of escape from reality, the most obvious among them being the candle. The doppelgänger of Alma, the glass menagerie of Laura, and the automobiles of Cassandra are other symbols of that escape.

Death, desertion, and decline surround these women, and they have been ever present in the lives of Williams' heroines. The age of chivalry, which has been romanticized to them in their youth, has disappeared. Their homes have been sold, their families have died, sickness and mental breakdown have been everywhere. Blanche says:

> All of those deaths! The lone parade to the graveyard! Father, mother! Margaret, that dreadful way! So big with it, it couldn't be put in a coffin! But had to be burned like rubbish! You just came home in time for funerals, Stella. And funerals are pretty compared to deaths. Funerals are quiet, but deaths— not always.

Along with a consciousness of general decay in her society, the early Williams heroine has undergone a far more violent experience, has known one particularly crucial bout with reality which has so terrified her that she refuses to see reality again. Blanche's husband committed suicide, a tragedy she had caused through a careless remark. Amanda's husband deserted her. Alma is jilted by young Doctor John. Cassandra watched her great-aunt die. And yet, paradoxically, these heroines try to recapture the past which has been one of death. In the past they were comparatively secure; they had their families for support, even though the various members of these families were slowly dying.

Seeing the romanticized past die before their very eyes, these heroines cling all the more firmly to the romantic aspect of it. The past thus represents at the same time a way of life which has been idealized to them in their childhood and death which has destroyed this way of life. Therefore, incapable of meeting the responsibilities that death has put before them in their later formative years, they consciously ignore the horrible aspects of the past and seek to embrace its careless, pleasant aspects in order to retain "the glory and the dream," that world of imagination which is peculiar to childhood; this accounts for the aura of all-pervasive immaturity which tends to make them seem less responsible for their acts than they really are. Blanche says:

> His Auntie knows that candles aren't safe, that candles burn out in little boys' and girls' eyes, or wind blows them out and after that happens, electric light bulbs go on and you see too plainly.

... There is little that is tragic about the early Williams heroines. They are sometimes intentionally comic, and often pathetic and melodramatic, but they never are tragic. Blanche and Amanda cannot be tragic figures because they have been defeated before their appearance on stage. We watch them grovelling before their fate, their machinations with destiny, their defeated pride, their illusions about themselves and their fellow man. We watch their attempts at compromise: Amanda, in choosing a husband for her daughter; Blanche in coming to stay with Stella. Amanda and Blanche, like Cassandra and Alma, become of interest mainly from a sociological standpoint. The tragedy of these women is the tragedy of the civilization which bore them, nourished them, and then cast them out. They are social fossils in an age of commercialism and tawdriness. Their defeat is the defeat of a culture which is, as Williams demonstrates, destroying itself, and which cannot brook the encroachments upon it. If we pity Blanche and Amanda, it is because they are beautifully portrayed examples of defeated human beings. They are living characters whose reactions to life and actions in life are familiar in one way or another to all of us. We may understand and pity them, but it is difficult for us to admire them as noble in any sense of the word. They are too weak, passive, and neurotic to be tragic.

CHAPTER 2

Themes and Characterization in *The Glass Menagerie*

READINGS ON
THE GLASS MENAGERIE

The Episodic Structure of *The Glass Menagerie*

Felicia Hardison Londré

Since *The Glass Menagerie* is composed of scenes from Tom's mind, Felicia Hardison Londré suggests that the play's episodic structure mirrors the selectivity and fragmentary nature of memory. The play's seven scenes are linked by lighting and recurring music. After summarizing the basic plot of each scene, Londré argues that in its broadest sense *The Glass Menagerie* is a dramatic poem about human nature.

Felicia Londré is a professor of theater and dramaturgy with the Missouri Repertory Theatre. She is an actress, set designer, and director of drama workshops. Her writings include *Tom Stoppard* and *Federico Garcia Lorca*.

The Glass Menagerie was Williams's first play to reach Broadway, and it was a triumph. Referring to the very different fortunes of this play and of *Battle of Angels* four years earlier, Williams reportedly said, "You can't mix sex and religion . . . but you can always write safely about mothers."

Although the characterization of the mother is generally perceived as unsympathetic, *The Glass Menagerie* is Williams's gentlest play. This is because the mother, Amanda Wingfield, and her daughter Laura are so isolated in their personal illusions of life. Amanda's son Tom, the narrator-protagonist, attempts to convey a sense of the harsh realistic background against which their story is set: "the slow and implacable fires of human desperation," hot swing music and liquor, labor disputes and economic depression in America, and Berchtesgaden and Guernica in Europe. But Tom is the only one of the three to make contact with that outer reality, and even he prefers the escapism of the movies.

THE PLAY'S STRUCTURE

The play is composed of scenes from Tom's memory, filtered through his remembered desire to escape from his mother's apartment and from his shoe-factory warehouse job, and through his implicit feelings of guilt for actually having abandoned his sister. "In the episodic play such as this," Williams wrote in his production notes, "the basic structure or narrative line may be obscured from the audience; the effect may seem fragmentary rather than architectural." This fragmentary quality is justified by the selectivity of memory and by the fact that each fragment is so finely chiselled. It is easy to see why Williams has been called a good "scenewright." So tightly written are the scenes in *The Glass Menagerie,* so full of musicality and suggestive power are the lines of dialogue, so integral are the effects of sound and lighting—that a summation of what is said and done on stage cannot nearly convey a sense of the play.

The formal division of the play consists of seven scenes. Scenes 1–5 are entitled "Preparation for a Gentleman Caller," and Scenes 6 and 7, "The Gentleman Calls." The scene divisions are not apparent to the audience, since most scenes are in turn composed of shorter episodes, and all segments are linked by changes in the lighting and by a "recurring tune, which dips in and out of the play as if it were carried on a wind that changes."

In Williams's original conception of the play, the setting was to incorporate a screen on which images and titles would be projected, to give emphasis to certain values in each episode. These images and titles are specified in library editions of the play (New Directions and most anthologies), but not in the acting edition (Dramatists Play Service). The screen device was not included in the original production, nor is it generally used, although it might be useful to enhance the conceptual unity of other nonrealistic elements of the play. For example, as if in answer to Tom's questioning the possibility of escape, the grinning wall photograph of his long-absent father lights up.

A PLOT SUMMARY

Tom begins the play by strolling onto the fire escape outside the Wingfields' St. Louis tenement apartment. He addresses the audience:

Yes, I have tricks in my pocket, I have things up my sleeve. But I am the opposite of a stage magician. He gives you illusion that has the appearance of truth. I give you truth in the pleasant disguise of illusion.

He explains that the play is memory. Then he enters the apartment as the lights come up on the interior. His first memory is of his mother Amanda thrusting upon her children the recollections and values of her long-lost way of life among the planters of the Mississippi Delta. She tells about the Sunday afternoon when she received seventeen gentlemen callers, and she tactlessly reproaches her daughter Laura for not having any.

Amanda learns that Laura has stopped going to classes at Rubicam's Business College because Laura is so shy about the brace she wears on one leg. Now that it is apparent that Laura will never be in a position to support herself, Amanda becomes obsessed with the idea of finding "some nice young man" to marry Laura. "Realizing that extra money would be needed to properly feather the nest and plume the bird," Amanda begins selling magazine subscriptions by telephone. Two of her hysterically eloquent sales pitches intersperse the action.

An argument with Tom brings forth more eloquence. One example is the speech in which she repeats the word "movies" and in which the "m" and "n" sounds take on the incantatory effect of poetry:

I don't believe that you go every night to the movies. Nobody goes to the movies night after night. Nobody in their right mind goes to the movies as often as you pretend to. People don't go to the movies at midnight, and movies don't let out at two A.M. Come in stumbling. Muttering to yourself like a maniac! You get three hours sleep and then go to work. Oh, I can picture the way you're doing down there. Moping, doping because you're in no condition.

Tom's anger builds to the point at which he calls his mother an "ugly—babbling old—*witch*" and hurls his coat across the room. His coat strikes the shelf that holds Laura's glass collection. Amanda exits, declaring that she will not speak to Tom again until he apologizes. Tom crosses the room and kneels to pick up the pieces of glass.

The next morning, in response to Laura's plea, Tom apologizes to Amanda. On speaking terms again, they nearly resume the same quarrel, but, with Laura sent out on an errand, Amanda succeeds in having Tom agree to bring home some nice young man from the warehouse to meet Laura.

After supper one evening, Tom casually tells Amanda that he is bringing someone home to dinner the following day. Amanda begins a flurry of questions about the young man's character, background, and prospects for the future. Tom cautions her that the gentleman caller doesn't know about Laura, nor should Amanda expect too much of Laura: "She lives in a world of little glass ornaments, Mother.... She plays old phonograph records and—that's about all—." He leaves for the movies. Amanda calls Laura from the kitchen to wish on the moon.

The dinner guest, Jim O'Connor, had been a high-school hero six years before. He was the boy whom Laura secretly liked in high school. At the warehouse, he is Tom's only friend. He knows of Tom's habit of retiring to the washroom to write poems on the lids of shoe boxes. When Laura learns that Jim is to be the guest, she becomes nervous and ill. She panics and bolts from the room after answering the door. Amanda appears, wearing a girlish frock resurrected from a trunk—the dress she was wearing when she met her husband. She lavishes her Southern charm on Jim and credits Laura with having cooked the dinner. Too ill to come to the table with the others, Laura is left lying on the living room sofa.

Just as dinner is ending, all the lights in the apartment go out; Tom had neglected to pay the electric bill. He and Amanda go to the kitchen, while Jim is sent into the parlor, carrying a candelabrum with lighted candles, to entertain Laura. Jim tells Laura about the courses he is taking for self-improvement and about his plans to get in on the ground floor of television and go right to the top with it. He judges her to be an "old-fashioned type of girl" which he thinks is "a pretty good type to be." Gradually, Jim draws her out, and, finally she shows him her collection of little glass animals.

Jim asks Laura to dance with him to the music coming from the Paradise Dance Hall across the alley. While dancing, they knock to the floor Laura's favorite glass animal—the unicorn. With its horn broken off, Laura assures Jim that it will feel less "freakish." Clearly, Jim has had this effect on Laura too. After he kisses her and then awkwardly apologizes, explaining that he cannot "do the right thing," cannot take down her phone number and "call up next week" because he is already engaged to be married, she gives him the hornless unicorn as a "souvenir."

Amanda enters with a pitcher of lemonade and learns of Jim's engagement. As soon as Jim has left, Amanda turns against Tom to reproach him for the fact that they had entertained "some other girl's fiancé." Tom starts to make his habitual escape to the movies, and Amanda says, "Go then! Go to the moon—you selfish dreamer!" And Tom tells the audience:

> I didn't go to the moon, I went much further—for time is the longest distance between two places. . . . I would have stopped, but I was pursued by something. It always came upon me unawares, taking me altogether by surprise. Perhaps it was a familiar bit of music. Perhaps it was only a piece of transparent glass. Perhaps I am walking along a street at night, in some strange city, before I have found companions. I pass the lighted window of a shop where perfume is sold. The window is filled with pieces of colored glass, tiny transparent bottles in delicate colors, like bits of shattered rainbow. Then all at once my sister touches my shoulder. I turn around and look into her eyes. Oh, Laura, Laura, I tried to leave you behind me, but I am more faithful than I intended to be! I reach for a cigarette, I cross the street, I run into the movies or a bar, I buy a drink, I speak to the nearest stranger—anything that can blow your candles out! . . . For nowadays the world is lit by lightning! Blow out your candles, Laura—and so goodbye.

THE PLAY AS A DRAMATIC POEM

The Glass Menagerie is sometimes called an expressionist play, but it is probably closer to symbolist drama, with its poetic language, suggestive interplay of *états d'âme,* and use of light and music to play upon the sensibilities. It has been called naturalistic, as well as Chekhovian. Like [Russian playwright, Anton] Chekhov's plays, it has been staged both as comedy and as tragedy. It sets up contrasts between the dreamer (Tom) and the doer (Jim), past and present, fantasy and actuality, desire for escape and awareness of responsibility, psychological and physical handicaps, a civilization "gone with the wind" and a world obsessed with technological progress. It can be seen as a play about conflict between generations, posing the question that Williams later articulated in his *Memoirs* and hinted at in several other plays: "Why do women bring children into the world and then destroy them?" Clive Barnes (*New York Times,* December 19, 1975) has called *The Glass Menagerie* a play about loss and survival. Roger B. Stein, in his essay *"The Glass Menagerie* Revisited: Catastrophe Without Violence" (in *Tennessee*

Williams: A Collection of Critical Essays), discusses its extensive religious imagery and symbolism. In broadest terms, *The Glass Menagerie* is a dramatic poem about human nature.

THE CRITICAL RECEPTION OF THE PLAY

The Glass Menagerie was first produced at the Civic Theater in Chicago on December 26, 1944, with set design and lighting by Jo Mielziner and original music composed by Paul Bowles. Eddie Dowling was producer and director, and he played the role of Tom. The role of Amanda was taken by Laurette Taylor, in a comeback after a long absence from the stage. She had virtually dropped out of sight after the death of her husband J. Hartley Manners in 1928, and was remembered most fondly for her creation of the title role in his play *Peg o' My Heart* in 1912. Her name was soon to become as closely associated with Amanda Wingfield as it had been, for an earlier generation of theatergoers, with Peg. In 1944, it was considered somewhat of a risk to cast her at all, but her rightness in the part became legendary.

Chicago critics wrote glowing reviews of the play and of its performers, but, perhaps because of the icy weather, the public ignored the production. After the first week's disappointing box office, Dowling and coproducer Louis J. Singer decided to close the play, but Chicago newspaper critics launched a crusade to save it. Claudia Cassidy, Ashton Stevens, Henry T. Murdock, and others used their daily columns to urge theatergoers not to let a work of art of such rare quality die in Chicago. The press used its power to good effect, for in the third week of its Chicago run, *The Glass Menagerie* began playing to full houses.

Illusion Versus Reality in *The Glass Menagerie*

Nilda G. Joven

Nilda Joven writes that the Wingfields, isolated in their apartment, live in an illusionary world: Amanda lives in the past, Laura lives in a fragile world of her glass collection, and Tom longs for adventure. The first three scenes of the play establish the fears and dreams of the isolated and friendless family. At the end of scene 3, the shattering of the glass menagerie foreshadows the collision of the Wingfield world of illusion with reality when Jim O'Connor, the gentleman caller, arrives for dinner. For Williams, Joven argues, illusions will inevitably shatter when confronted with reality, but they are nevertheless beautiful.

The beauty of the illusions, particularly Laura's world, is made poetic and charming as it is filtered through the memory of Tom. Joven discusses how Williams uses light and music to enhance the beauty of Tom's memory. Light, for example, helps create a touching image of Laura as she is bathed in pools of soft and clear light recalling a Madonna portrait.

Nilda G. Joven is a faculty member in the Department of Speech and Drama at the University of the Philippines.

Williams' first award-winning play was *The Glass Menagerie*, which won three awards in 1945. He has since become a significant playwright in the American theatre. The world of Williams' plays is one of loneliness and violence. It is peopled with characters who are soft, fragile, odd, or desperate. Their driving passion is generally the desire to escape the chaos and corruption about them, or the terrifying world of reality.

From "Illusion and Reality in Tennessee Williams' *The Glass Menagerie*," by Nilda Joven, *Diliman Review*, vol. 19, no. 1 (January 1966), pp. 81–89. Reprinted by permission of the *Diliman Review*.

The Glass Menagerie dramatizes one aspect of the conflict between illusion and reality, a theme that preoccupies Williams in his plays.

THE WINGFIELDS' ILLUSIONARY WORLD

As always with Williams, illusion is viewed kindly in the play. The Wingfields live in their own private worlds that are far removed from reality, hugging closely hopes for the future, occasionally engaging in pathetic attempts to make them come true.

Amanda lives in the past, in her world of jonquils and gentlemen callers. She is presented as out of touch with reality; she is flighty, and a source of embarrassment to her children. However, she is genuinely concerned about securing her crippled daughter's future.

The crippled Laura is abnormally shy. She spends her time washing and polishing her glass collection and playing music on the Victrola. She has had to drop out of school and business college because her extreme self-consciousness has made it impossible for her to cope with problems like examinations. But Tom does not see Laura as queer. Memory colors his picture of her, and he makes us equate Laura, as he does, with fragility and delicate beauty.

Tom, the poet, dreams of running away to a life at sea, to get away from his stifling job at the warehouse. He quarrels with his mother and stays out late at night against her wishes. But the conflict he feels between his desire for adventure and his duty towards Laura and his mother makes him a sympathetic character. Even the absent father, the "telephone man who fell in love with long distances", makes his charming presence felt from the smiling blown-up photograph over the mantel.

Another character in the play, Jim O'Connor, the gentleman caller, represents reality. Through him Williams pokes fun at reality, which he judges less sharply in this play than in later ones. Jim O'Connor, the outsider, the stumble-John, is the high school hero who didn't do very well after school, but still likes to give out free advice as though he knew all the answers. He is good-natured, but a bit of a lout. He chews gum after meals, pauses to admire his shadow while stretching, and explains to Laura, as he takes the gum out, how he is going to wrap it up in a piece of paper so it won't get stuck on a shoe. He tries to get Laura out of her shell, but only succeeds in shattering her world by drawing her out, kissing her, then telling her that he's engaged.

The illusion-reality conflict in the play arises from the untenability of the Wingfield position in the modern era in which they live: "Knowledge—Zzzzzp! Money—Zzzzzp!—Power! That is the cycle democracy is built on!"

The Wingfields cannot co-exist with the real world around them because to live as they wish is to deny the existence of such a world. Amanda's dreams deny the passage of time. Laura's life denies the outside world completely. This is what makes her situation more difficult than Amanda's, for the latter at least acknowledges the need of some means of support to continue living in a competitive society.

The ironic impact of the plays comes with Amanda's manipulation of the events that lead to a confrontation between the Wingfields and the outside world. To live, it is necessary either to go into the outside world, or find someone in the outside world to support Laura. Either process means her destruction.

THE ISOLATION OF THE WINGFIELDS

Amanda's fantasies are revealed in the first scene that immediately follows Tom's introduction to the play. Amanda, Tom, and Laura are having dinner, all through which Amanda nags Tom about the way he eats. Laura rises to get the blancmange for dessert. Amanda tells her to resume her seat so that she can stay "fresh and pretty—for gentlemen callers." Laura tells her that she is not expecting any callers, but Amanda says that sometimes they come when they are least expected. This starts her talking about one Sunday in Blue Mountain when she received seventeen gentlemen callers. It is obviously an oft-repeated story, for Tom exclaims, "I know what's coming!" after she mentions "one Sunday afternoon in Blue Mountain". It is a wistful story as she remembers it, so many fine southern gentlemen she could have married, and she chose their father!

The scene ends with Laura's apologetic comment to Tom, "Mother's afraid I'm going to be an old maid." This recalls another scene to Tom's mind, through which we are made aware of Laura's extreme shyness and of the fact that she is crippled. Amanda comes home after having discovered that although Laura has apparently been regularly going to business college for the last six weeks, she actually dropped out after the first speed test. She had been so nervous, she threw up on the floor. And rather than either go back or tell her mother that she was dropping out, she had gone to parks, museums, and glass houses during the hours when she was supposed to be at business college. Amanda soon gets over her shock and starts thinking of other plans for Laura. She suggests marriage. Laura's reaction is one of fright, "But, Mother, I'm crippled."

That Tom feels he is in some way responsible for the eventual shattering of the worlds of Amanda and Laura is revealed in the next scene. Tom's anger has been aroused by Amanda's constant intrusion on his privacy. She censors the books he reads, returning to the library those which she believes unsuitable. She interrupts him while he is at his typewriter, attempting some creative work. The quarrel extends to the hours he says he spends at the movies. Amanda finds it difficult to believe that he stays out till the early hours of the morning every night, just going to movies. He taunts her with her worst fears. Exaggerating them he tells her sneeringly, "My enemies plan to dynamite this place. They're going to blow us all sky-high some night! I'll be glad and so will you! You'll go up on a broomstick, over Blue Mountain with seventeen gentlemen callers! You ugly—babbling old—witch . . ." He then leaves the room. On his way out, he hurls away the coat he has been struggling to put on. It strikes the shelf of Laura's collection. Laura screams, "My glass!—menagerie . . ."

These first three scenes show the dreams and fears that set the Wingfields apart from the world of reality. The Wingfields live in an apartment building. But they do not seem to have friends among their neighbors. Amanda sometimes works to supplement the family income, but the jobs that she takes do not involve working with other people. She was a demonstrator at a department store. When she solicited magazine subscriptions, she did it by phone. She is a member of the D.A.R. [Daughters of the American Revolution], but doesn't seem to have made friends this way, either. Laura stays at home most of the time. The attempt to put her through business college was a failure. When she did go out at the time she was supposed to be going to the college, she went to parks, museums, and glass houses where she did not have to talk to people. Even Tom, who worked at a warehouse, made no friends. He was on friendly terms with Jim

O'Connor only because, as he put it, "I was valuable to him as someone who could remember his former glory." The other workers in the warehouse were suspicious of him because when business was slack, he would closet himself away in a cabinet in the washroom, writing poetry.

THE WINGFIELD COLLISION WITH REALITY

The shattering of Laura's glass menagerie at the end of scene three foreshadows what will happen to the Wingfields when they finally have to face reality. The need to do so comes with Amanda's realization that no gentlemen callers will drop in unexpectedly nor can she become a career woman. She makes other plans to provide for Laura's future. If no gentlemen caller will come to call, then someone must be invited over to dinner to meet Laura. Amanda, the unrealistic one, feels that an introduction like this will suffice to solve the problem of finding Laura a suitable husband. Even as she discusses Laura with Tom, we see how impossibly out of touch with the rest of the world she is as the conversation drifts back to Tom's restlessness. Tom tries to explain his restlessness by saying, "Man is by instinct a lover, a hunter, a fighter, and none of these instincts are given much play at the warehouse." Amanda will not hear of the word "instinct" applied to men, "Instinct is something that people have got away from! It belongs to animals! Christian adults don't want it!"

After Amanda's talk with Tom, he invites Jim O'Connor to dinner. Amanda cross examines her son about the visitor as though the young man had already asked to marry Laura. Tom tries to warn her that Jim doesn't even know about Laura. He tells her not to expect much of Laura, who is crippled and different from other girls. Amanda will not allow the word "crippled" to be used. She maintains, besides, that the difference (between Laura and the other girls) is all to Laura's advantage.

Tom's answer shows that he, at least, has some hold on reality. "Not quite all—in the eyes of others—strangers—she's terribly shy and lives in a world of her own and those things make her seem a little peculiar to people outside the house."

For the second time in the play Laura is then identified with the glass menagerie, as Tom elaborates, "She lives in a world of her own—a world of—little glass ornaments, Mother. . . . She plays old phonograph records and—that's about all—."

But Amanda dismisses Tom's misgivings and prepares for the dinner guest by taking out the floor lamp she has started making payments on, placing new curtains on the windows, new chintz covers and throw pillows on the chairs and sofa. She makes Laura a new dress.

Laura is very pretty, the house is in readiness, but Amanda's eccentricity will not allow her to stop there. She resurrects the dress she used to receive her gentlemen callers in, to relive once again the glorious days of her girlhood. The situation is made more unpropitious when Laura discovers the name of the visitor. Jim O'Connor is the high school boy she had secretly liked in college, a matter she has earlier confided to her mother. She begins to feel sick in the stomach and becomes too ill to have dinner with the family.

The final scene is a tender one. In Tom's mind, it glows like the candles that light the scene. In this scene, Laura's identification with the glass menagerie is further underlined. This time she is specifically identified with her favorite piece, the unicorn. Jim's lines foreshadow again what is to happen to Laura, "Unicorns, aren't they extinct in this modern world?"

But for a brief while after Laura shows Jim her glass collection, we are made to feel that perhaps Jim might bring Laura out of her shell after all. He dances with her, succeeds in making her laugh and relax. He kisses her, and at this point might have changed the course of her life. But stumble-John that he is, he tells her that he shouldn't have done that, that he will not call again because he is engaged.

Amanda blames Tom for this final fiasco—he might have bothered to find out whether Jim was engaged before inviting him home. The scene fades out with Tom threatening to leave and Amanda telling him to go to the moon. The play ends as it began, with Tom, the narrator, this time saying good-bye to his memories of Laura.

THE BEAUTY AND VULNERABILITY OF ILLUSIONS

In *The Glass Menagerie* the shattering of illusion is poignant. The play dramatizes illusion's encounter with reality. It shows clearly that the Wingfields, particularly Laura, have little chances of survival in what Jim O'Connor terms "the cycle democracy is built on". It records an observation that, confronted with reality, illusion falls apart. But it suggests that illusion can be beautiful, reality dull.

When this is so, the destruction of illusion is poignant, the triumph of reality unwelcome.

To dramatize this view of illusion and reality, Williams uses a device which Tom speaks of after the opening lines of *The Glass Menagerie*, "The play is memory. Being a memory play, it is dimly lighted, it is sentimental, it is not realistic." Tom's memory lights the past as the lamp does the bits of colored glass in the window of the shop where perfume is sold. Seen through the poet's eye, scenes from his past take on the charm of "bits of shattered rainbow".

Memory surrounds Laura with a delicate glow, an almost ethereal beauty. She is seen through lighting that recalls religious portraits of the Madonna. In Williams' production notes to the play, he states, "In keeping with the atmosphere of memory, the stage is dim. Shafts of light are focused on selected areas or actors, sometimes in contradistinction to what is the apparent centre. For instance, in the quarrel scene between Tom and Amanda, in which Laura takes no active part, the clearest pool of light is on her figure. . . . The light upon Laura should be distinct from the others, having a peculiar pristine clarity such as light used in early religious portraits of female saints or Madonnas."

The kind of light Williams describes is first used to light only Laura's face. The background is the faded tapestry of the living room curtains. The subject being discussed is gentlemen callers. The light shines on Laura's face as she listens to her mother's protestations. "It isn't a flood, it isn't a tornado, Mother. I'm just not popular like you were in Blue Mountain. . . ." The scene is sentimental, but it is also a touching portrait, acceptable as a brother's memory of his sister.

It is in the quarrel scene mentioned by Williams that the next special lighting effect on Laura is used. Her face is again specially lighted at the beginning of the last scene. The stage directions envision the desired effect thus: "As the curtain rises Laura is still huddled upon the sofa, her feet drawn under her, her head resting on a pale blue pillow, her eyes wide and mysteriously watchful. The new floor lamp with its shade of rose-colored silk gives a soft, becoming light to her face, bringing out the fragile, unearthly prettiness which usually escapes attention." Here again is the imagery of the Madonna and of the "bits of shattered rainbow" that the poet identifies with his sister.

Finally, Tom remembers Laura as framed in candlelight.

There is reference to Jim's smile lighting Laura "inwardly with altar candles." The candles sustain the Madonna imagery. They also serve to strengthen the word imagery of Laura's life being snuffed out, which is the effect the scene leaves on us.

Less dramatically special lighting is also occasionally used on Amanda. A spot of light isolates her from the scene as she loses herself in her memories of her former suitors. In the scene after her quarrel with Tom, Williams sees her as standing "rigidly facing the window on the gloomy grey vault of the areaway. Its light on her face with its aged but childish features is cruelly sharp, satirical as a Daumier[1] print."

The memory play device not only makes it possible to make lighting a major dramatic tool. It also enlists the help of music. As Tom claims, "In memory everything seems to happen to music." This may appear quite a weak excuse for the use of music in the play, but these particular memories may have been genuinely triggered off by music in anyone's mind, because one of the two things that Laura occupies herself with is playing old phonograph records. The music for the play is a single recurring tune which resembles circus music heard from a distance when one "is thinking of something else." Heard under these circumstances Williams believes that it "expresses the surface vivacity of life with the underlying strain of immutable and inexpressible sorrow. When you look at a piece of delicately spun glass you think of two things: how beautiful it is and how easily it can be broken. Both of those ideas should be woven into the recurring tune, which dips in and out of the play as if it were carried on a wind that changes."

Conceived thus, it is played during Tom's narration and from there through most of the play. It is supplemented by music that Laura plays on the Victrola when she wants to escape unpleasant situations. She plays it when her mother confronts her with her having dropped out of business college. She also plays it to gain time before answering the door when Tom brings the gentleman caller home. She plays it after Jim O'Connor takes his leave. One piece of music indicated the effect of which I am dubious about because it is so pointedly and obviously insinuated is the "Ave Maria" in the

1. French painter, Honoré

same scene after the quarrel when Williams sees Amanda as a Daumier print.

Across the alley from the Wingfield apartment is a dance hall. Music from the dance hall is heard when Tom talks about the cramped, unwholesome atmosphere of their neighborhood, and through the scene when Tom discusses the gentleman caller with Amanda. This underlines the ironic disparity between Amanda's enchantment over the prospect of a gentleman caller and the disenchantment of the dance hall. The music from the Paradise Dance Hall is heard again when Jim O'Connor tells Amanda and Laura about his girlfriend, Betty. It goes right on after Amanda tells Tom, "Go then! Then go to the moon—you selfish dreamer!"

Since the entire play is seen through Tom Wingfield's point of view, the associations he makes as a poet also strengthen the illusion of delicate beauty. It is Tom the poet who associates Laura with bits of colored glass and with familiar phrases of music. It is the poet's mind which perceives the ironic contrast between the hopes of Amanda and Laura and the harsh reality of Paradise Dance Hall. It is also Tom's mind, strongly biased in favor of his family that draws such a caricature of Jim O'Connor.

Like Tom, Williams is also a poet. He writes strong scenes that show great insight into a world of special people. But in most of his plays, these scenes, like the Marguerite–Don Juan scene in *Camino Real* or Val's description of the blue bird to Lady in *Orpheus Descending,* remain isolated scenes. In these instances, Williams fails to achieve an organic unity between strong scenes and the rest of the play. In *The Glass Menagerie,* however, the memory play device provides a happy medium for Williams' talents. Each scene of the play is a poetic statement about the glass menagerie which was the Wingfield household. Framed as the scenes are in memory and unified by the statement they make about the menagerie, they constitute an organic wholeness which is not achieved in other plays of Williams.

The Character of Amanda Wingfiel

Alice Griffin

Alice Griffin argues that Amanda Wingfield clings to an illusion of herself as a beautiful belle in an elegant Old South, where, by her own account, she was pursued by countless suitors. Through the course of the play, Amanda represents the futility of trying to re-create the past. Caught in an illusion of her own making, she cannot accept her children as they really are. At times, Amanda overwhelms Laura and Tom with her endless and breathless talking. However, despite Amanda's self-deception, Griffin supports the notion that she does not live entirely in the past, and that she is sensitive to the fragile condition of her family and the desperation of their current situation.

Alice Griffin is a theater editor and critic. She has broadcast radio literary reviews for WNYL and WBAI in New York City and taught drama studies at Lehman College in New York City.

Amanda Wingfield is the first in a line of memorable women Williams will create, and, like the others, she is a many-faceted, unique individual. But Amanda is also a universal type, a mother with the characteristic qualities of devotion to her offspring and determination to survive for their sakes. She is, however, an extremist who carries these traits to their limits, and beyond. She may, like all mothers, nag Tom to eat more and Laura to do her homework, but only Amanda can chirp so cheerfully each morning, "Rise and shine!" to her weary son or urge him, in scene 1, "chew—chew! Animals have secretions in their stomachs which enable them to digest food without mastication, but human beings are supposed to chew their food before they swallow it down."

Although the family now lives in reduced circumstances in St. Louis on Tom's salary of sixty-five dollars a month as a warehouse clerk, Amanda never stops reminding her children of her own more affluent past. Reminiscing is a recognizable parental characteristic, but it is an obsession with Amanda. In his introduction to "The Characters" Williams says she is "clinging frantically to another time and place."

AMANDA'S ILLUSION OF HERSELF

Retreating from the harsh reality of the Depression to the illusion of herself in the legendary Old South of elegant beaux and belles makes the present somehow more bearable for Amanda. Laura understands this, as she begs Tom, impatient with his mother's oft-told tale, to "let her tell it. . . . She loves to tell it," as Amanda in scene 1 launches into the first of her arias about the past: "One Sunday afternoon in Blue Mountain—your mother received—*seventeen!*—gentlemen callers! . . . My callers were gentlemen—all! Among my callers were some of the most prominent young planters of the Mississippi Delta—planters and sons of planters!" The myth of the Old South, in which Amanda devoutly believes, was one of gracious living, family tradition, chivalry, and coquetry which lent a stability of time and place to those who partook of it, as Thomas E. Porter points out. Alienation from place led to the "preoccupation with time" which affects Amanda as she constantly harks back to earlier days.

Strangely anachronistic in a 1930s tenement, Amanda's airs and graces are those of a woman brought up only to look attractive, behave graciously, and choose a husband from among many suitors. Although in her recollections she is sought after by many eligible young men (ironically, she tells Tom that "character" is important in choosing a mate), these happy courting days ended sadly. Unfortunately, her upbringing did not prepare her to choose a mate for qualities other than "charm," nor did it train her to earn her own living when her charming spouse deserted her. To supplement Tom's meager salary she has demonstrated brassieres at a department store for the fifty dollars' tuition for Laura at business school and now sells magazine subscriptions by phone to decorate the apartment for the expected dinner guest.

Despite her lapses into her earlier, more glorious days, Amanda does not live in the past—a luxury she could not afford. She recognizes that their situation is near desperate, but she is unable to accept Tom and Laura as they are. Laura is crippled, though Amanda insists on never allowing "that word to be used!" Tom, who hates his warehouse job, wants only to be left alone to write, but Amanda refuses to recognize or accept his creative work or even the books he reads: "That hideous book by that insane Mr. Lawrence. . . . I cannot control the output of diseased minds. . . . BUT I WON'T ALLOW SUCH FILTH BROUGHT INTO MY HOUSE!" (sc. 3). Tom's escape is to go to the movies, a pastime Amanda resents. As Williams introduces Amanda in "The Characters," he notes that "there is much to admire in Amanda, and as much to love and pity as there is to laugh at. Certainly she has endurance and a kind of heroism, and though her foolishness makes her unwittingly cruel at times, there is tenderness in her slight person."

AMANDA'S VALOR

In New York PM Magazine, *writer Joan Evans recounts a conversation she had with Tennessee Williams about the character of Amanda.*

I asked Mr. Williams if he always wrote about unhappy, trapped, hopeless people. He'd been half-reclining against a pillow on his bed, but he sat up now.

"I hadn't thought of them as being hopeless," he said. "That's not really what I was writing about. It's human valor that moves me. The one dominant theme in most of my writings, the most magnificent thing in all human nature, is valor—and endurance.

"The mother's valor is the *core* of *The Glass Menagerie,*" he went on. "She's confused, pathetic, even stupid, but everything has *got* to be all right. She fights to make it that way in the only way she knows how."

Delma Presley sees Amanda, along with Laura and even Jim, as "characters caught up in illusions of their own making": "All of them . . . have built their lives on insubstantial premises of deception." And it is Amanda "who always seems to reap the bitter consequences of deception," by her husband, by Laura (in going to the zoo instead of business school), by Tom (in using the light bill money to join the merchant seamen), and even, unwittingly, by the gentleman caller. One must keep in mind, however, that Amanda, despite her urging "gay deceivers" (bosom enhancers) upon

Laura in scene 6, deceives no one except perhaps herself, for she really believes in her role as a Southern belle.

The visual image and its implications were as important to Williams as his dialogue: "When I write, everything is visual, as brilliantly as if it were on a lit stage." In scene 6 Amanda becomes a touching visual image of the futility of attempting to recreate the past in the present. Although she is now twice the age of the belle she was, she dons for the invited gentleman caller a "girlish frock of yellowed voile with a blue silk sash," which she found in an old trunk, wears her hair in ringlets, and carries a bunch of jonquils to revive the "legend of her youth . . . nearly." With dinner guest Jim, as if he were her suitor, she behaves with "girlish Southern vivacity . . . social charm . . . gay laughter and chatter." The vignette is as gently humorous as it is pathetic.

AMANDA'S SPEECH PATTERN

As he will do with his future heroines, Williams gives Amanda a distinctive idiom. Her two long speeches to Jim in scene 6 are characteristic: "I've heard so much about you from my boy. I finally said to him, Tom—good gracious!—why don't you bring this paragon to supper? I'd like to meet this nice young man at the warehouse!—instead of just hearing him sing your praises so much! I don't know why my son is so stand-offish—that's not Southern behavior!" (Southern behavior in Amanda's view evidently did not value facts as much as style.) After one word from Jim and four from Tom, she expands on her "gracious living . . . gentlemen callers . . . sons of planters" and marriage to a man who "travels and I don't even know where!" She is breathlessly loquacious, as if endless talking could stave off an unexpected Caller, who might just be gentlemanly enough to wait until she has finished.

Because most of his heroines are Southern, Williams can heighten what he observes to be the "natural eloquence" of Southern women. In Amanda's speeches critic Stark Young hears "the echo of great literature." Fearing Laura will be a spinster, Amanda in scene 2 onomatopoetically describes such women as "little birdlike women without any nest—eating the crust of humility all their life." The rhythm and meter in Amanda's speeches are often that of iambic pentameter: "Laura, come here and make a wish on the moon! . . . / A little silver slipper of a moon" (sc. 5).

Although annoying at the time, Amanda's excesses can be viewed in retrospect by Tom with gentle humor—her self-dramatizing in scene 2 with Laura over her leaving the business college, her coquettish manner with Jim, and her two phone conversations. Amanda is at her best (and worst) in the telephone calls to Daughters of the American Revolution (DAR) friends to promote magazine subscriptions that might bring in extra money "to feather the nest and plume the bird," as Tom says. But in scene 3, beneath her gushing descriptions of the serial fiction—"a book that critics already compare to *Gone with the Wind*"—one senses a note of desperation.

Loneliness in
The Glass Menagerie

Winifred L. Dusenbury

According to Winifred L. Dusenbury, socioeconomic
conditions have prevented the Wingfields from making any meaningful connections, to one another or
other people, and hence they are doomed to loneliness. Laura's paralyzing shyness, her lameness, and
her mother's pressure have left her incapable of any
kind of meaningful personal interaction. She retreats
further and further from reality into a world of glass
figures and phonograph records.

Amanda is also removed from the world around
her and to cope with her isolation she projects her
past into the present. At the play's end, Amanda's
loneliness is complete when Tom leaves and Laura
withdraws into herself. Tom physically escapes the
isolation he feels at home and moves into the world
of reality when he joins the merchant marine, but,
Dusenbury argues, Tom's last lines indicate that he
not yet found a sense of belonging.

Winifred Dusenbury is a professor of English at
the University of Florida, Gainesville. Her works
include (under the name of Winifred Dusenbury
Frazer) *Love as Death in "The Iceman Cometh"* and
Emma Goldman and "The Iceman Cometh." She contributes articles on modern drama to professional
journals and magazines.

Several American dramatists have made valuable contribu-
tions to the modern theatre in plays portraying the isolating
effects of the particular socioeconomic conditions of the
South. Tennessee Williams, frequently an interpreter of the
lonely Southern female who lives in romantic dreams of the
past but is lost in the modern world, has written two prize-

winning plays on the theme: *The Glass Menagerie,* which won the Critics Circle Award for the season 1944–45; and *A Streetcar Named Desire,* which won both the Critics Circle Award and Pulitzer Prize for 1947–48. Although Lillian Hellman's theme in *The Little Foxes* (1939) and *Another Part of the Forest* (1946) is the rapaciousness of a family of rising Southerners, she contrasts them with the ruined aristocracy who now belong nowhere, but who play an important part in the dramas. Paul Green, in a number of plays, notable among which is *The House of Connelly* (1931), has portrayed the loneliness of decay into which the old Southern plantation owners have fallen. All three playwrights emphasize the changing social and economic structure as the basis for a kind of personal near-annihilation of those Southern aristocrats who cannot adapt themselves to changing conditions, and a sense of belonging to those who can. . . .

The symbolism of *The Glass Menagerie,* which is a memory play evoked in the mind of Tom, the son and narrator, is carried partly in the title; for the family is like the glass collection in the frowsy apartment, ill-adapted to its environment. The playwright says of Laura, the shy daughter who has a slightly crippled leg,

> Stemming from this [defect], Laura's separation increases till she is like a piece of her own glass collection, too exquisitely fragile to move from the shelf. (Author's Production Note)

Tennessee Williams further advises that the light, which should not appear realistic, should descend in a shaft upon Laura in several scenes in which she is only the onlooker, "with a peculiar pristine clarity such as light used in early religious portraits of female saints or madonnas." Laura's "separation" is thus symbolically illustrated by the lighting and staging. Nathan calls her "a creature crippled deeply in inner spirit," and it is certain that her physical disability is small compared to her psychological isolation.

LAURA'S LONELINESS

It is no wonder that Laura suffers from a painful sense of loneliness, for from the first scene to the last, her mother makes her feel her lack of popularity with men and her inability to cope with any kind of social life. Laura's closing line of the first scene, "Mother's afraid that I'm going to be an old maid," is complemented by the closing scene in which the gentleman caller departs, never to return. In the

WILLIAMS'S PERSONAL SENSE OF LONELINESS
In his memoirs Williams identifies loneliness as his own greatest affliction—an affliction that shapes both his life and his work.

As to this particular friend who occupied the center of my life from the late fall of 1946 till at least half a year later, and who continues to be among the closest of my friends, let me only say, now, that he relieved me, during that period, of my greatest affliction, which is perhaps the major theme of my writings, the affliction of loneliness that follows me like my shadow, a very ponderous shadow too heavy to drag after me all of my days and nights.

intervening action Laura's pitiful inner apartness from the life around her is made overt by other incidents. Amanda's lack of sympathy of the girl's nervous sickness at business school elicits only Laura's reply of "I couldn't face it. I couldn't." Any contact with people is almost more than Laura can face. Seemingly her only sense of attachment is to her little glass figures, but this feeling of closeness to them is so intense that when Tom throws his coat and accidentally knocks some off the shelf, she cries out "as if wounded," and covers her face with her hands. Her devotion to so fragile a material object as the glass menagerie represents the enervation of her spiritual connection to anything. She substitutes playing the old phonograph records and dusting the figures in her menagerie for a healthy interest in living. As Tom says, "She lives in a world of her own," which is so unrelated to that of those around her that she seems "peculiar." When left alone with the gentleman caller, her speech is low and breathless from her paralyzing shyness. For a few moments with the young man, Jim, she comes into accord, as he displays a "warmth and charm which lights her inwardly with altar candles," but the scene increases the pathos of Laura's situation, for it ends by Jim's announcement that he is to be married to a girl named Betty. The humiliation of the rebuff would seem likely to stand in the way of her ever again even approaching a state of understanding with another individual.

To make Laura's sense of separateness doubly explicit, the playwright has inserted into the scene between Jim and Laura stage business with a little unicorn, her favorite figure. Since it has a horn and is different from all the horses, Jim remarks, "Poor little fellow must feel kind of lonesome." Although Laura insists he gets along well with the horses, it is with deep feeling that she says, after the horn has been broken by a fall,

> He's lost his horn. It doesn't matter. Maybe it's a blessing in disguise. . . . The horn was removed to make him feel less— freakish! Now he will feel more at home with the other horses, the ones who don't have horns.

Laura's "horn" is the slight limp, which she has magnified to make her seem to herself "a freak," until she has become in a sense just that. Knowing how alone she is and always will be, Tom, although he must run away to save himself, is forever haunted by a feeling of guilt towards her and pleads that her candles may be extinguished in his memory. As the final curtain falls, Laura blows out the candles, and having thus apparently been forgotten by Tom, is left in black lone-liness forever.

Laura has created around herself something of the at-mosphere which [German novelist] Thomas Mann explains in "The Making of 'The Magic Mountain.'" Speaking of the tuberculosis sanitarium, he points out "the dangers of such a milieu for young people," and the idea expressed in his book "of the narrowness of this charmed circle of isolation and invalidism," which makes the patient "become com-pletely incapable of life in the 'flatland.'" Laura lives in a mountainous retreat of her own making and has thus lived for so long that she is now incapable of life among the vale of people. Unlike Amanda, she has no past to which she can belong, and, as Tom recognizes, she obviously has no future to which she can look forward, so she exists from day to day, avoiding reality by withdrawing into herself, spending her lonely days dusting her little glass animals.

AMANDA'S LONELINESS

Amanda is a pitiful, even a tragic, figure according to Ten-nessee Williams. As Tom gives his closing speech of the play and the light is upon the pantomime of Amanda comforting Laura, the playwright says of Amanda: "Now that we cannot hear the mother's speech, her silliness is gone and she has dignity and tragic beauty." Her slow, graceful gestures indi-cate her upbringing in a genteel tradition. Circumstances have put her in a position that makes her reminiscences of the past ridiculous, but Jim, the gentleman caller, is sincere in toasting "the Old South" with her, for she has quite charmed him by her chatter, which although it seems affected to the audience, has an air of authenticity and warmth to the visitor. Amanda's taking out her feeling of dissatisfaction with herself upon Tom finally drives him away and leaves her alone with Laura, whose withdrawal makes companionship impossible. "Amanda," says Tennessee Williams, "having failed to establish contact with reality, continues to live vitally in her illusions." Since she is so removed from the world around her, Amanda is able, to some extent, to belong to the past, even going so far as to believe herself "girlish." Pitiful as is such adherence, however, she is not so alone as Laura, because of her ability to project the past into the present and be a part of it.

Amanda never sees the irony of her position. Although it is the charm of her husband which has led to his departure, the "cultivation of charm" should be Laura's aim in life. Even as the photograph of the smiling, but missing, head of the household is illuminated by a spotlight and as Amanda admits, "That's the only thing your father had plenty of—charm!" still she is urging Laura, "You have to cultivate charm—or vivacity—or charm!" Occasionally, though, her imagination fails, and Amanda feels lost, as when she appeals to Tom to help get a suitor for Laura. "In these trying times we live in," she pleads, "all that we have to cling to is—each other." "Clinging" best describes her relationship to her present life and "remembering," to her past. Whether the pathos of her life is important enough to be tragic is doubted by many critics. Alan Downer says of Tennessee Williams' plays that "though his themes are in possibility tragic, his plays are in actuality pathetic. Each of his characters passionately resists the moment of illumination, rejects the self-knowledge which might give tragic dignity to her failure." If there is real tragedy in Laura and Amanda and others of Williams' characters whose world has been wrecked by changing social conditions, perhaps it is the very fact that they do not have any recognition of their failure. If their heredity is such that they not only cannot adapt to a different status in life but also cannot come to any understanding of their situation, the tragedy is perhaps one of the whole society from which they are derived. Is it not tragic that Southern society has produced such characters, who, whether typical of mankind or not, are apparently typical of

their class? This is to ask, of course, whether Aristotle's definition of tragedy should be revised for twentieth-century
America. Is "social tragedy" an anomalous term?

TOM'S LONELINESS

Tom is lonely like his mother and Laura, but he is not a pathetic figure and surely not a tragic one, except insofar as his
escape from the "coffin" of his home is possible only in a
physical sense. But on the literal level, Tom's escape is
heroic and successful. George Kernodle cites it as one example of a happy escape from the strangling arms of home
and family. This critic believes that the theme of escape is
one of the most common in modern drama because of the
deterministic cynicism of the twentieth century, which has
left no other solution. In the mind of the audience Tom, like
his father, is more than justified in running away, for as he
says, "I haven't got a thing, not a single thing left in this
house that I can call my own." He complains justly about his
"2 by 4 situation," which, like being nailed in a coffin, cuts
him off entirely from all contacts. Tom has a recognition,
too, of the family's plight, which the women lack, for he
points out that Jim is "an emissary from a world that we
were somehow set apart from." Tom does escape from the
isolation which he feels in his home by going into the great
world of reality—the Merchant Marine, and although his
closing lines indicate that he does not find a sense of belonging in "motion," perhaps he has made an advance toward it by breaking the bonds which tied him to his mother.

Tennessee Williams' description of his scene for *The Glass
Menagerie* might be that of *Street Scene*. Like [*Street Scene*'s
author] Elmer Rice he makes explicit in the stage directions
that it is the mass of humanity, which is unable to provide
any sense of identity to its individual members, which
makes tenement living so lonely. He explains that the Wingfield family lives in

> one of those vast hive-like conglomerations of cellular living-
> units that flower as warty growths in over-crowded urban
> centers of lower middle-class population and are sympto-
> matic of the impulse of this largest and fundamentally en-
> slaved section of American society to avoid fluidity and dif-
> ferentiation and to exist and function as one interfused mass
> of automatism.

Amanda, it must be admitted, shows a certain courage in

refusing to become one with the mass by maintaining her illusions, for there is perhaps more hope in living in the past than in being submerged in the present, and Laura likewise manages to keep some iota of identity through her glass menagerie. Tom escapes from this interfusion of mankind, as well as from his family, and attains some individuality by traversing the globe. As a whole, however, socioeconomic conditions have left all the Wingfields unattached to a satisfactory object of devotion and doomed them all to loneliness.

The Glass Menagerie as Social Commentary

Thomas Allen Greenfield

According to Thomas Allen Greenfield, *The Glass Menagerie* portrays the conflict between a world of repetitive and meaningless work and an individual's desire for passion and romance. The play attacks work by revealing the toll the economic system takes on the human spirit. Greenfield discusses Williams's belief that work that is tedious and deadening denies the passion and impulsiveness that is at the core of human nature. Tom Wingfield resists this deadening process by rejecting Amanda's pressure to conform and by scorning Jim's faith in the gods of shallow appearances, upward mobility, and ambition. Tom is a poetic soul and a restless spirit who flees from Jim's life of tedium and the dysfunctional society that supports it.

Thomas Allen Greenfield is a professor of English and dean of the College of Arts and Sciences at Bellarmine College, Louisville, Kentucky. He is also a national board member of the Federation of State Humanities Councils.

The emergence of Tennessee Williams at the same time as Arthur Miller has invited comparisons between them. While the differences between their dramatic styles and literary themes have been duly noted by many drama critics, the two playwrights have some similar insights into the state of the modern America, insights that are all the more intriguing because of the very different artists who share them. In his essay "American Blues..." Kenneth Tynan notes that Williams's and Miller's early works have shared two "joint ventures": their criticism of the "familiar ogre of commercialism, the killer of values and the leveller of men" and modern man's frustration. "Techniques change, but grand

Reprinted from *Work and the Work Ethic in American Drama, 1920–1970*, by Thomas A. Greenfield, by permission of the University of Missouri Press. Copyright ©1982 by the Curators of the University of Missouri.

themes do not. Whether in a murder trial, a bullfight, a farce like *Charley's Aunt* or a tragedy like *Lear,* the behavior of a human being at the end of his tether is the common denominator of all drama." What Tynan fails to mention is that these two "joint ventures" can be seen as a shared response, political and visceral, to work in America. For in his play *The Glass Menagerie* Williams presents us with an irresolvable conflict between meaningless, rationalized modern work and the passion and romance that are for Williams the life's blood of men who are intellectually and spiritually alive.

We see an early treatment of this theme in Williams's short play *Moony's Kid Don't Cry* (1940). Moony, a semi-articulate but somehow poetic factory worker, understands completely how modern factory work is grinding up his spirit as well as the souls of his oblivious fellow workers:

> I look at tings diffrunt. . . . Other guys—you know how it is—they don't care. They eat, they drink, they sleep with their women. . . . The sun keeps rising and Saturday night they get paid . . . [and] someday they kick off. . . . My God, Jane. I want something more than just that.

Irritated by his wife's capitulation to their oppression and meaningless existence ("There *ain't* no more than just that"), Moony lapses into an angry, violent escape fantasy. Invoking the spirit of independence of the pre-industrial age craftsmen who owned their own labor and found meaning in their work, Moony longs to do something significant with his hands:

> [My hands] are so kind of empty and useless. . . . I feel like I oughta be doin' something with these two hands of mine besides what I'm doin' now—runnin' bolts through an everlastin' chain.

But since he cannot, he dreams of taking an axe into his hand and of smashing away at the "Smoke, whistles, plants, factories, buildings, buildings buildings" to get to where "it's clear." The fantasy, which ends abruptly when his baby cries in the next room, combines the spirit of the independent pioneer woodsman and the anger of the proletarian revolutionary. However, unlike Tom Wingfield in *Menagerie,* Moony cannot bring himself to act upon his intense desires to escape.

THE PLAY AS SOCIAL COMMENTARY

Although the impressionistic technique, the declaration of the drama as a "memory play," and the haunting relationship between Tom and Laura tend to distract attention from the play's social commentary, *The Glass Menagerie* contains as straightforward an attack on the modern system of work and the middle class that succumbs to it as can be found anywhere in postwar American drama:

> I turn back time to that quaint period, the thirties, when the huge middle class of America was matriculating in a school for the blind. Their eyes had failed them or they had failed their eyes, and so they were having their fingers pressed forcibly down on the fiery Braille alphabet of a dissolving economy. In Spain there was revolution. Here there was only shouting and confusion. In Spain there was Guernica. Here there were disturbances of labor.

Yet Williams, like Miller, is far more interested in the toll that such an economic system takes upon the human spirit and the ability to live a life that is meaningful, dignified, and passionate than he is in the "fairness" of one system of economics or another:

> The Wingfield apartment is in the rear of the building, one of those vast hive-like conglomerations of cellular living that flower as warty growths in overcrowded urban centers of lower middle-class population and are symptomatic of the impulse of this largest and fundamentally enslaved section of American society to avoid fluidity and differentiation and to exist and function as one interfused mass of automatism.

Although Tom seems to dismiss the social context of the drama as merely "the social background of the play," Williams does not, as we quickly learn in Tom's confrontations with his mother. To Williams, Amanda represents the dying but not quite dead pre-industrial work values of rural America, both in her inability to understand the emptiness in her own life and in her insistence that Tom surrender his rebellious lust for adventure in the name of conformity to traditional values of self-reliance, self-sacrifice, and hard work:

AMANDA. Most young men find adventures in their careers.

TOM. Then most young men are not employed in a warehouse.

AMANDA. The world is full of young men employed in warehouses and offices and factories.

TOM. Do all of them find adventures in their careers?

AMANDA. They do or they do without it. Not everybody has a craze for adventure.

TOM. Man is by instinct a lover, a hunter, and fighter, and none of these instincts are given much play at the warehouse.

AMANDA. Man is by instinct! Don't quote instinct to me! Instinct is something that people have got away from! It belongs to animals. Christian adults don't want it.

As in [Miller's] *Death of a Salesman,* the world of work represents a threat to the very essence of man. Williams perceives man to be a passionate, instinctive, impulsive being who is denied this crucial dimension of his humanity by being forced to work at something tedious and respectable. The tedium of the warehouse job causes a crisis in Tom's life that is so deep it breaks down his not inconsiderable sense of obligation to his mother and even penetrates his intense love for his sister, Laura.

THE WINGFIELDS' ATTITUDE TOWARD WORK

If Tom is the irrepressible romantic who will not be held by the constraints of an aging society's fading work ethic, Laura is that society's most helpless prisoner. A physical cripple, she is also a societal cripple for she cannot, as her mother so insidiously reminds her, bring herself to cope with the task of learning a job skill:

AMANDA (TO LAURA). So what are we going to do the rest of our lives. Stay home and watch the parades go by? Amuse ourselves with the glass menageric, darling? Eternally play those worn out phonographs your father left as a painful reminder of him? We won't have a business career—we've given that up because it gave us indigestion.

Tom is too strong to succumb to society's demands on working, self-sufficient, upwardly mobile young people, but Laura is too weak either to resist or to accept those demands. She cannot work, but she cannot defy the practical necessity of work. She does not escape by fighting but by playing with her fragile glass figurines within the prison of her mother's house. But she is linked to Tom for she too is the child of a man who found no happiness in Amanda Wingfield's joyless house of self-discipline, responsibility, and bourgeois social climbing. And as the last remaining family prisoner of Amanda's empty value system, she is finally called upon by Tom to "blow out the candles," to blot out that time and place from his memory.

It might not have been necessary for Tom to escape from his mother's house and way of life if her values were to die with her. But through Jim, the gentleman caller, we learn that the gods of success, upward mobility, and ambition have been passed to a new generation, fully equipped with the gizmos and gadgets of twentieth-century technology. His faith in shallow appearances and personality manipulation

WILLIAMS'S EARLY WORK EXPERIENCE

In his memoirs Williams discusses the comradeship that he felt working with other minimal-salaried workers at Continental Shoemakers. *This early work experience helped shape Williams's socialist political views.*

When I came home, Dad announced that he could no longer afford to keep me in college and that he was getting me a job in a branch of the International Shoe Company.

This job was to last for three years, from 1931 to 1934. I received the wage of sixty-five dollars a month—it was the depression.

Well, truly, I would take nothing for those three years because I learned, during them, just how disgraceful, to the corporations, is the fate of the white-collar worker.

I got the job because Dad had procured for the top boss his position at the Continental Shoemakers branch. . . . Of course the bosses were anxious to find an excuse to get me out. They put me to the most tedious and arduous jobs. I had to dust off hundreds of shoes in the sample rooms every morning; then I had to spend several hours typing out factory orders. Digits, nothing but digits! About four in the afternoon, I was dispatched to the establishment of our main client, J.C. Penney, with great packing cases of shoes for their acceptance or rejection. The cases were so heavy that it was a strain to lift them: I could carry them only half a block before having to set them down to catch my breath.

Still, I learned a lot there about the comradeship between co-workers at minimal salary, and I made some very good friends, especially a Polish fellow named Eddie, who sort of took me under his wing, and a girl named Doretta, with whom Eddie was infatuated. Then there was the spinster at the desk next to mine, little plump Nora. While we worked we carried on whispered conversations about the good movies and stage shows in town and the radio shows such as "Amos and Andy."

My first year there I came of age and I registered and I cast my first and last political vote. It was for Norman Thomas: I had already turned Socialist, and for reasons already made clear.

is strikingly similar to Willy Loman's and perfectly compatible with Amanda's:

> Primarily it amounts to—social poise! Being able to square up to people and hold your own on any social level.

But unlike Amanda, whose faith in traditional, rural work values is grounded in a dying past, Jim's faith in work and success is aimed at the future. He explains his philosophy while telling Laura of his visit to the Century of Progress exhibit in Chicago:

> What impressed me most was the Hall of Science. Gives you an idea of what the future will be in America, even more wonderful than the present time.

Because he is the first gentleman caller Laura has ever had, Jim represents a romantic hope to Amanda. But symbolically his values represent the hope for the survival of her own values of hard work, self-sacrifice, and voluntary enslavement to the work system; she sees him as a role model for Tom, a caretaker for Laura, and a savior for herself. But just as his values hold out a false hope for a wonderful America, he holds out a false hope to Amanda Wingfield. Totally mistaken in his assessment of Laura's real needs, tolerant but uncomprehending of Tom's love for adventure, and virtually oblivious to his own problems, Jim is David Riesman's outerdirected man: soulless, and image conscious, he seeks only to talk, to sell, and to "zzzzzzzp" his way from "the ground floor" to "the top."

WILLIAMS'S CONDEMNATION OF SOCIETY

This searing social commentary on American working life stops short of being a realistic drama, for memory, magic, and the turning back of time allow for the triumph of Tom Wingfield's poetic soul and restless spirit. In a fit of rage after discovering that Jim is engaged to be married, Amanda tells Tom to "go to the moon." Tom responds with a triumphant, final dash down the fire escape that renders the world of conformity, hard work, and familial responsibility a distant if painful memory:

> I didn't go to the moon. I went much further. . . . I descended the steps of this fire-escape for the last time and followed, from then on, in my father's footsteps, attempting to find in motion what was lost in space—I traveled around a great deal. The cities swept about me like dead leaves, leaves that were brightly colored but torn away from the branches. . . .

> Then all at once my sister touches my shoulder, I turn around
> and look into her eyes. . . . Oh Laura, Laura, I tried to leave
> you behind me, but I am more faithful than I intended to be.

Although *The Glass Menagerie* is more concerned with a man's memory of his family than it is with his memory of his job, the work from which Tom flees is more than a mere catalyst for his rejection of the past. It is the link between his family and the larger society, both of which trap him and confine him to a world that has stripped itself of its poetry and imagination. Tom's perspective of the values of work upheld by Amanda and Jim is the greatest obstacle to an existence that is meaningful and dignified. Willy Loman [in *Salesman*] and Joe Keller [in *All My Sons*] share Tom's view in this respect.

What distinguishes Tom from Willy and Joe is that he is aware of the danger to him that lies in his mother's values and attitudes toward work. Moreover, he is able to substitute an alternative set of values and act upon them. This difference suggests that Williams sees man as free to walk away from his society and its constrictions whereas Miller clearly sees man as a being that cannot survive outside of his society. Unlike Tom, Willy and Joe must come to terms with their working lives, or die trying. This difference further suggests that, at least in this play, Williams condemns his society as hopeless, moribund, and disfunctional. But for Miller there is the hope and belief that society can reform itself; characters like Bernard, Charlie, and Chris Keller hold out for society the hope that social adjustment is possible without the loss of principle, self-worth, or self-knowledge. It is not an easy adjustment, for there will always be men like Joe Keller and Willy Loman, and society itself will continue to invite common and even uncommon men to make mistakes. But Miller believes that both the society and the men who live in it are vital, and thus capable of adjusting to one another. His is the role of the social physician, probing and analyzing the living society in front of him. On the other hand, Williams seems to adopt the role of the anthropologist in *The Glass Menagerie*. He examines from a distance the ruins of Amanda's dead civilization. Psychological probing gives way to a sense of detached curiosity, as if Williams were trying to restore a small measure of life and movement to mummies and skeletons.

Tom's Soliloquies

Thomas L. King

Thomas L. King argues that *The Glass Menagerie* is built on Tom's soliloquies, or dramatic monologues. The typical production emphasis on Amanda rather than Tom is a distortion that began with the first staging of the play in 1945, when the director, Eddie Dowling, highlighted the actress Laurette Taylor as the mother. King believes that the play belongs to Tom—after all, the characters and even the setting are aspects of Tom's consciousness.

Tom, like Williams himself, is an artist who must distance himself from the debilitating atmosphere of his family and reality to maintain his creativity. King believes that Tom's soliloquies reflect this distancing as they oscillate between sentimental memories and the ironic interruptions that keep him from being controlled by the past. King explains that Tom's ironic detachment is conveyed in his wit, mockery, and cockiness. In his last soliloquy at the end of the play, Tom departs not only from Amanda and Laura, but also from the audience, ironically exorcising his pain but leaving it with playgoers.

Thomas King is professor of English at Sweet Briar College in Virginia. He is a director and has acted in three stagings of *The Glass Menagerie.*

Tennessee Williams' *The Glass Menagerie,* though it has achieved a firmly established position in the canon of American plays, is often distorted, if not misunderstood, by readers, directors, and audiences. The distortion results from an overemphasis on the scenes involving Laura and Amanda and their plight, so that the play becomes a sentimental tract on the trapped misery of two women in St. Louis. This leads to the neglect of Tom's soliloquies—speeches that can be ignored or discounted only at great peril, since they occupy such a

Excerpted from "Irony and Distance in *The Glass Menagerie*," by Thomas L. King, *Educational Theatre Journal*, vol. 25, no. 2 (May 1973), pp. 207–14. Copyright ©1973 by the American Theatre Association, Inc. Reprinted by permission of the Johns Hopkins University Press. Footnotes in the original have been omitted here.

prominent position in the play. When not largely igr
are in danger of being treated as nostalgic yearnin
mer time. But they are not sentimental excursions in
past, paralleling Amanda's, for while they contain sentiment
and nostalgia, they also evince a pervasive humor and irony
and, indeed, form and contain the entire play.   *Conclusion*

DISTORTION OF THE PLAY

Judging from the reviews, the distortion of the play began
with the original production. The reviews deal almost
wholly with Laurette Taylor's performance, making Amanda
seem to be the principal character, and nearly ignore the soliloquies. Even the passage of time has failed to correct this
tendency, for many later writers also force the play out of
focus by pushing Amanda forward. Among the original reviewers, Stark Young was one of the few who recognized that
the play is Tom's when he said "The story . . . all happens in
the son's mind long afterward." He also recognized that the
production and Laurette Taylor tended to obscure the script,
for, after a lengthy discussion of Miss Taylor, he said, "But
true as all this may be of Miss Taylor, we must not let that
blind us to the case of the play itself and of the whole occasion." Young blamed on [director] Eddie Dowling the failure
of the narration noted by others: "He speaks his Narrator
scenes plainly and serviceably by which, I think, they are
made to seem to be a mistake on the playwright's part, a mistake to include them at all; for they seem extraneous and
tiresome in the midst of the play's emotional current. If these
speeches were spoken with variety, impulse and intensity
. . . the whole thing would be another matter, truly a part of
the story." Young indicates that while the reviewers tended to
neglect Tom and the soliloquies to concentrate on Laurette
Taylor, they were encouraged to do so by a production which
made the play Amanda's.

TOM AS THE CENTRAL CHARACTER

The play, however, is not Amanda's. Amanda is a striking
and a powerful character, but the play is Tom's. Tom opens
the play and he closes it; he also opens the second act and
two further scenes in the first act—his is the first word and
the last. Indeed, Amanda, Laura, and the Gentleman Caller
do not appear in the play at all as separate characters. In a
sense, as Stark Young noted, Tom is the only character in the

play, for we see not the characters but Tom's memory of them—Amanda and the rest are merely aspects of Tom's consciousness. Tom's St. Louis is not an objective one, but a solipsist's created by Tom, the artist-magician, and containing Amanda, Laura, and the Gentleman Caller. Tom is the Prospero [or conjurer, from Shakespeare's *The Tempest*]of *The Glass Menagerie,* and its world is the world of Tom's mind even more than *Death of a Salesman*'s is the world of Willy Loman's mind. The play is warped and distorted when any influence gives Amanda, Laura, or the glass menagerie any undue prominence. If Amanda looms large, she looms large in Tom's mind, not in her own right; though of course the image that finally dominates Tom's mind is that of Laura and the glass menagerie.

The full meaning of the scenes between the soliloquies lies not in themselves alone but also in the commentary provided by Tom standing outside the scenes and speaking with reasonable candor to the audience and reader. Moreover, the comment that the soliloquies make is not a sentimental one; that is, they are not only expressions of a wistful nostalgia for the lost, doomed world of Amanda, Laura, and the glass menagerie but also contain a good deal of irony and humor which work in the opposite direction. They reveal Tom as an artist figure whose utterances show how the artist creates, using the raw material of his own life.

TOM'S ARTISTIC NATURE

The nature of the narrator's role as artist figure is indicated by Tom's behavior in the scenes. He protects himself from the savage in-fighting in the apartment by maintaining distance between himself and the pain of the situation through irony. For example, when he gets into a fight with Amanda in the third scene and launches into a long, ironic, and even humorous tirade—about how he "runs a string of cat-houses in the valley," how they call him "Killer, Killer Wingfield," how, on some occasions, he wears green whiskers—the irony is heavy and propels him out of the painful situation, out of the argument, and ultimately to the movies. Significantly, this scene begins with Tom writing, Tom the artist, and in it we see how the artistic sensibility turns a painful situation into "art" by using distance. In his verbal assault on his mother, Tom "creates" Killer Wingfield. Tom's ability to distance his experience, to protect himself from the debilitating atmosphere of the apartment makes him different from Laura. Laura does not have this refuge; she is unable to detach herself completely from the situation and she is destroyed by it. She does, of course, retreat to the glass menagerie and the Victrola, but this is the behavior of a severely disturbed woman. Her method of dealing with the situation, retreating into a "world of her own," does indeed, as Tom says, make her seem "just a little bit peculiar." Tom's method is more acceptable; he makes art.

The kind of contrast that exists between Laura and Tom is illustrated by a comment [psychoanalyst Carl] Jung made about James Joyce and his daughter, Lucia. Lucia had had a history of severe mental problems and, in 1934, she was put under the care of Jung. Discussing his patient and her famous father in a letter, Jung wrote: "His [Joyce's] 'psychological' style is definitely schizophrenic, with the difference, however, that the ordinary patient cannot help himself talking and thinking in such a way, while Joyce willed it and moreover developed it with all his creative forces, which incidentally explains why he himself did not go over the border. But his daughter did, because she was not a genius like her father, but merely a victim of her disease." On another occasion Jung said that the father and daughter "were like two people going to the bottom of a river, one falling and the other diving." We see here a psychoanalyst's perception of the problem of artist and non-artist which is much the same as the problem of Tom and Laura. Tennessee Williams' real-life sister, Rose, has also suffered from mental disturbances.

That an author's early play should contain a highly autobiographical character who shows the mechanism by which art is made out of the material of one's life is not particularly surprising, but it is a generally unnoted feature of *The Glass Menagerie* which is inextricably linked to the irony of the soliloquies. For the artist, irony is a device that protects him from the pain of his experience so that he may use it objectively in his art. We may suppose that [Jonathan] Swift's irony shielded him from the dark view that he had of the world and that the failure of that irony brought on the madness that affected him at the end of his life. The artist needs his distance from the material of his art so that he may handle it objectively, and the soliloquies of *The Glass Menagerie*, in part, reveal the nature of that distance and how it is maintained.

Generally, each soliloquy oscillates between a sentimental

memory of the past, which draws the narrator into it, and a wry irony which keeps him from being fully engulfed and controlled by it. This tension is found in all the soliloquies, though it is not always handled in the same way: sometimes the fond memory is predominant and sometimes the irony, but both are always present. At times, Tom seems almost deliberately to court disaster by creating for himself and the audience a memory so lovely and poignant that the pain of giving it up to return to reality is too much to bear, but return he does with mockery and a kind of wit that interrupts the witchery of memory just short of a withdrawn madness surrounded by soft music and a mind filled with "delicate rainbow colors." In short, Tom toys with the same madness in which his sister Laura is trapped but saves himself with irony. . . .

TOM'S MANIPULATION OF THE AUDIENCE

The culmination of all the soliloquies and of the tension between irony and nostalgia that is carefully developed in them, is in the final one. Tom's last speech contains just two touches of ironic detachment, but these are critical and are the foci on which this speech and, indeed, for Tom, the whole play turns. The speech begins with a touch of ironic humor. In the preceding scene, Amanda has told Tom to go to the moon. He begins his final speech with "I didn't go to the moon." This is a decidedly humorous line, indicating that Tom still has access to his detachment, but the audience is not laughing anymore, its detachment has been broken down. The speech then quickly moves into a tone of lyric regret:

> I didn't go to the moon, I went much further—for time is the longest distance between two places—
>
> Not long after that I was fired for writing a poem on the lid of a shoe-box.
>
> I left Saint Louis. I descended the steps of this fire-escape for a last time and followed, from then on, in my father's footsteps, attempting to find in motion what was lost in space—
>
> I traveled around a great deal. The cities swept about me like dead leaves, leaves that were brightly colored but torn away from the branches.
>
> I would have stopped, but I was pursued by something.
>
> It always came upon me unawares, taking me altogether by surprise. Perhaps it was a familiar bit of music. Perhaps it was only a piece of transparent glass—

Perhaps I am walking along a street at night, in some strange city, before I have found companions. I pass the lighted window of a shop where perfume is sold. The window is filled with pieces of colored glass, tiny transparent bottles in delicate colors, like bits of a shattered rainbow.

Then all at once my sister touches my shoulder. I turn around and look into her eyes . . .

Oh, Laura, Laura, I tried to leave you behind me, but I am more faithful than I intended to be!

I reach for a cigarette, I cross the street, I run into the movies or a bar, I buy a drink, I speak to the nearest stranger—anything that can blow your candles out!

—for nowadays the world is lit by lightning! Blow out your candles, Laura—and so good-bye.

The irony in this passage is no longer humorous. When Tom says "I didn't go to the moon," no one is laughing, and the final, ironic "and so good-bye" is not even potentially humorous. Tom seems to have been captured by the memory and the audience has almost certainly been captured, but Tom, in the end, still has his detachment. Laura's candles go out and Tom is relieved of his burden, uttering a final, flip farewell, but the audience has been more faithful than it intended to be; they are left behind, tricked by Tom who is free for the moment while they must face their grief, their cruelty, for they are the world that the Wingfields were somehow set apart from, they are the ones who shattered the rainbow.

The soliloquies, then, are of a piece: they all alternate between sentiment and irony, between mockery and nostalgic regret, and they all end with an ironic tag, which, in most cases, is potentially humorous. They show us the artist manipulating his audience, seeming to be manipulated himself to draw them in, but in the end resuming once more his detached stance. When Tom departs, the audience is left with Laura and Amanda alone before the dead, smoking candles, and Tom escapes into his artist's detachment having exorcized the pain with the creation of the play. This is the trick that Tom has in his pocket.

The Search for Freedom in *The Glass Menagerie*

V. Rama Murthy

The central theme of *The Glass Menagerie* is the conflict between Tom's personal need for freedom and
his love for his family. V. Rama Murthy argues that
this central theme carries the tragedy of the play. He
writes that it is tragic not in the old sense, following
the dictates established by Aristotle, but rather in a
modern way. Tom knows the ramifications of his
leaving; he understands the tragic suffering and guilt
that will result from his flight, but he chooses to
leave believing that love can only sustain itself in an
atmosphere of freedom. Hence, Williams takes a
simple domestic situation and turns it into a conflict
of tragic dimensions.

V. Rama Murthy is a professor of American literature at Kurukshetra University in Delhi, India.

The Glass Menagerie is autobiographical and Williams has
drawn the characters from his own mother, sister, his father
and one of his friends.

Tom Wingfield and his sister with their mother were deserted by their father who "fell in love with long distances".
Laura is a girl who is psychologically withdrawn from life
because of her crippled state and the futility of her early
'crush' on a fellow high school student. She does not do well
in her examinations, in business education either. Tom,
whose interest is poetry finds his job at the shoe factory incompatible with his nature. He is persuaded by his mother
Amanda to bring home a nice young man from the factory
. . . a gentleman caller . . . who might prove a beau for Laura.
The gentleman caller is Jim O'Connor who successfully
breaks Laura's reserve and instils hope, love, and confi-

Reprinted from *American Expressionistic Drama* by V. Rama Murthy (Delhi, India:
Doaba House, 1970).

dence in her. While leaving their house he discloses to
that he is engaged to be married very soon. This upsets
Amanda and Laura and the young lady relapses into her former dream world.

THE CHARACTER OF AMANDA

The character of Amanda dominates the whole play. She is,
"a little woman of great but confused vitality clinging frantically to another time and place." Her characterization must
be carefully created, not copied from type. She is not paranoic, but her life is paranoia. There is much to admire in
Amanda and as much to love and pity as there is to laugh at
her. She is a sweet mother, a pathetic creature and at the
same time a disgusting shrew. Certainly she has endurance
and a kind of heroism, and though her foolishness makes
her unwittingly cruel at times, there is tenderness in her
slight person. "The peculiar difficulty that Amanda has to
face is that she has to act the role of father as well as
mother." In her conversation with O'Connor she exhibits a
vivacity that her own children lack. In guiding her daughter
she recalls her own past as a girl and therefore is a little out
of tune with the times of her own children. She tries to be
practical in her romantic girlishness. Though her disposi-
tion is romantic she has not yet recovered from the shock
her husband gave her by deserting them. She wants to be
prudent now and she wants her children to be realistic. She
tells Tom that the future becomes the present, the present
the past, and the past turns to everlasting regret if one does
not plan for it. She is, however, unable to free herself of the
illusions in which she grew.

She is shrewish, nagging and sometimes vulgar. She is an
aged coquette and a foolish dreamer. With all this, she is a
woman of courage and endurance. When she finds that the
gentleman caller affair has ended in a fiasco—she does not
lose heart. But towards the end when she comforts her daughter she acquires a "tragic dignity and tragic beauty." If she has
not been so petulant and if she has resigned herself to fate a
little, she should not have suffered so much and troubled her
son so much. Her petulance makes her look ridiculous.

THE CHARACTER OF LAURA

The plight of Laura is given a luminous expression. Her limp
is responsible for the whole tragedy. She, too, like her

brother, has a poetic soul. She is unable to adapt herself to the business college education and therefore she lives in a world of candle light and fantasy. She spends her time polishing the tiny glass animals and listening to her father's old phonograph records. Like Tom, she hated the work of the machine age and could never learn to type. For a while she believes her mother's world and does not resist when Jim kisses her. At once she becomes hopeful of her future. But very soon Jim's disclosure of his intending marriage with Betty shatters her hopes. The playwright seems to feel, as Benjamin Nelson points out, that beauty and delicacy cannot long survive in the world of reality. The beauty and gentility of Laura make her an anachronism which gets smashed up in the harsh world outside the glass menagerie. Laura who is like a "piece of translucent glass touched by light is too fragile to stand the strain of life. Her radiance is a momentary radiance, not actual, not lasting." For a moment Jim comes nearer Laura's heart but soon realizes that he cannot take and preserve his ambitious dreams. He recoils and rationalizes his diffidence and uncertainty by remembering that he is engaged to Betty (a figure that may contribute to his success).

Jim and Amanda have a lot in common with each other as Tom and Laura have. Like Amanda, Jim too moves with a mask of success. With all his dash and brilliance he finds himself in the same warehouse in which Tom works. Tom and Laura know what they want in life and they are not after worldly success. But Jim is a part of the American dream. He wants to be in the forefront of the successful man and he is after shallow success. He is really an emissary from another world totally free from the dreams and fears of the Wingfield family.

THE CHARACTER OF TOM

The character of Tom provides the key to the play's theme. Amanda's lecture on practical wisdom disgusts Tom. He hates his mother's morning song "Rise and shine". He knows that his mother's excessive enthusiasm will only make their lives awkward. He loves both his mother and sister but he is not in a position to help them. Only by escaping from them and getting into the wide world he can find a solution for their lives. But his pity for his mother and his sympathy for his sister hold him back. For a while he tries to believe in the practical wisdom of his mother and brings Jim home but soon realizes that his mother is foolish. Tom's disinterest or unconcern is forced upon him by the helpless state in which he is himself caught up.

Like [Eugene] O'Neill, Tennessee Williams in *The Glass Menagerie* is an anarchist. There is a purposeful disintegration of the family in the play. Critics have called Tom and his father irresponsible people but they serve to illustrate the author's idea of the need of freedom. He does not treat Tom's father with harshness even though that man is responsible for the anguish of the whole family. Tom has the lineaments of his father and he follows his foot-steps to satisfy and realize his inner aspirations. The persons who are entirely dependent and who stand in the way of his freedom are the two women. Laura, the sick girl, is a burden on Tom. She preys on his freedom not willfully but by right of convention of family life. Amanda, though affectionate as mother, is insensitive to Tom's anxiety. "What right have you to jeopardize your job?" she asks him. "Jeopardize the security of us all? How do you think we'd manage if you were. . . ."

Williams's characters bring degradation on themselves willfully and knowingly. It is not brought on by 'chance' or 'accident' or 'destiny'. They do not pose as innocent victims of an unseen fate. They fully accept their responsibility and suffer from one personal crisis to another and they do not murmur about it.

THE CENTRAL THEME IN *THE GLASS MENAGERIE*

The Glass Menagerie is a bold play with a very bold theme. It is the emancipation of man from his family ties. The critics who have not grasped this anarchist tendency in the play have interpreted it in various ways applying old standards. Benjamin Nelson says: "The story of Laura and Jim is simple and poignant, but it is neither the sole nor the central conflict in the play. Laura's personal dilemma is part of a greater dilemma; the destruction . . . slow and remorseless . . . of a family. It is not a melodramatic destruction; there is no battle of angels above them. It is gradual, oblique, and laced with pathos and humour, but is the erosion of a family nonetheless."

Benjamin Nelson thinks that the play presents genuine situation and motivation but it has a weakness and it lies in the playwright's "hardening philosophical commitment". According to him, the play is not a tragedy. For every one in the play "is a failure and in the course of their drama they all perish a little." None of these plays, according to him, are given the opportunity to triumph against fate which is "as malignant as it is implacable. Their struggle is a rearguard action against life, a continuous retreat. This retreat may be moving, pathetic, melodramatic, boisterous, but it is always withdrawal." And he concludes: "Their struggles, their hopes, and even their eventual destruction can never move far beyond pathos. The beauty and magic of *The Glass Menagerie* is that this pathos is genuine, objective and deeply moving." Benjamin Nelson in denying the tragic value to the play seems to do so through the spectacles of Aristotle. The concept of tragedy has radically changed and it has become a more comprehensive term. Like the . . . hero in *The Flies* [by French philosopher John-Paul Sartre] Tom leaves his family. No murder or rape or suicide takes place as the climax for the play. Tom has not been driven out by gods. It is just a self-imposed punishment on himself. No battle of angels is fought over his head. He perfectly well knows the extent of crime he is committing and he is also aware of the terrible feeling of guilt he has to bear throughout his life. But for this emancipation he will do anything. He tears himself away from people whom he loves so dearly. This calls for rare courage and conviction and inflicts a terrible tragic suffering on him.

The playwright has surely succeeded in projecting a delicate and sympathetic and genuine situation on the stage with the necessary objectivity required for it. The simple domestic situation acquires tragic dimensions here. The fact that the characters are not able to cope with their circumstances add a poignant note to the play. Their struggle ends in surrender and their confrontation with life ends in retreat on withdrawal.

Tom is the worst sufferer in the play. He is hurt by the insensitivity of the people both outside and inside his home. His mother expects everything from him as a matter of right. The world too expects the same from him. He is asked to sacrifice his higher aspirations for their lower cravings. He carries eternal anguish within him by leaving his family.

The central theme of the play seems to be the conflict between personal freedom and love and Williams seems to prefer the former because the latter cannot subsist without the other. Love can sustain itself only in an atmosphere of freedom.

The Role of the Family in *The Glass Menagerie*

Tom Scanlan

Tom Scanlan distinguishes two forces that drive *The Glass Menagerie:* Tom's desire to escape his family and Amanda's desire to hold it together, particularly to establish some kind of life for Tom's sister, Laura. Both Tom and Laura are fragile, sensitive people who are unable to withstand or tolerate the harsh necessities of life. Scanlan writes that Williams emphasizes Laura's specialness by comparing her with Jim, the gentleman caller. Jim is naive, with a blind belief in self-improvement and the American Dream. He thinks that he can cure Laura of her shyness but only manages to make things worse, symbolized by his awkward tumble into the glass menagerie. Jim returns to the workaday world and Laura is left in a mystical world outside of reality.

According to Scanlan, Williams has sympathy for the Wingfields' struggle against the world, a struggle that they will lose. The playwright provides the audience personal glimpses into the private relationships of the family as it looks out on the social world outside of their apartment. But Williams never allows the play to get sentimental. He uses humor and a mocking tone to pull the audience back from the family's pain, alternately embracing the characters and laughing at them, empathizing and sympathizing with them.

Tom Scanlan has taught modern drama at Lincoln University and George Washington University. He has published articles in various periodicals, including the *Virginia Quarterly Review.*

The major dilemmas of family life are imbedded in the dramatic action of Williams's plays, and the ideal that haunts

From *Family, Drama, and American Dreams* by Tom Scanlan. Copyright ©1978 by Tom Scanlan. Reproduced with permission of Greenwood Publishing Group, Inc., Westport, Connecticut.

his characters is family-related. Moreover, those plays which have been most successful artistically have been those mostly about the family—the plays up through *Cat on a Hot Tin Roof; Camino Real* is the only exception.

In the earlier plays Williams dramatized the family world in a state of collapse; in later ones family collapse is antecedent to the action. These two situations are combined in *The Glass Menagerie,* Williams's first successful play (and probably his most popular one). The play is a perfect fusion of the two subjects and so is a figure for Williams's entire career. In it the family is long lost and, also, we witness its struggle before it is lost. Williams captures the poignancy of family memories in a way all his own, without sacrificing the core of dramatic conflict which makes such memories less static.

The play is a prime example of Williams's artistry in establishing the relation between his own dramatic world and the conventions of realistic domestic drama to which his audience owes great allegiance, as he well knew. The play occurs in the mind of Tom Wingfield, who drifts in and out of the action both as narrator and participant in a peculiarly appropriate way. From the moment at the beginning when the scrim of the tenement wall dissolves and we enter the Wingfield's apartment, we are reminded of the household of so many family plays. The realistic convention of the fourth wall is evoked as Tom remembers his family.

Tom's evocation is self-conscious, for as "stage manager" he has control over the setting. But Tom is also at the mercy of his memories and irresistibly must relive them. The play keeps us poised between these two styles, these two times, throughout. This is, in fact, its strongest and most subtle conflict. Like Tom, we are continually tempted into the world of a realistic family struggle, but never allowed to enter it completely. The projections and lighting keep the effect slightly stylized during the scenes, the fragmented structure blocks us from too long an absorption in the action, and the reappearance of Tom as narrator forces us back to the present. It is Tom's final reappearance in this role, when the action of the memory play is completed, which releases the tension created between the two styles and dramatizes, in a final rush of emotion, the irretrievable loss of the family which Tom can never escape.

Tom cannot shake the memory of his family from his

mind; the dissolution of time and space in the play—that is, in his consciousness—heightens the importance of what he is remembering to make it the most significant thing about his existence. What he remembers—the bulk of the play—centers around two lines of action. The first is his desire to escape from his family just as his father had done before him: "He was a telephone man who fell in love with long distances." Tom, a would-be writer, is caught between a domineering mother and a stultifying warehouse job. He escapes to the porch, to the movies, to the saloon. And finally, in the end, we learn that he has followed his father out into long distances. The second line of action, the principal one, concerns his mother, Amanda, and her attempts to establish some kind of life for Tom's crippled sister, Laura. Amanda pins her hopes on getting "sister" married, after Laura fails because of painful shyness to continue in business school. A "gentleman caller" is found, Jim O'Conner, "an emissary from the world of reality," but all of Amanda's hopes are crushed as he turns out to be already engaged.

The plot is slight stuff, as Williams himself knew. The effect of the play derives in part from the contrast between its two lines of action. Amanda is given over to memories of her past life of happiness as a young southern debutante in Blue Mountain, Mississippi, where on one incredible Sunday she had seventeen gentlemen callers. She imitates the manners and graciousness of those days, a faintly ludicrous parody of southern gentility, the played-out tradition of the antebellum South and its family of security. But she has spirit, too, and responds to the problems of raising two children in a St. Louis tenement during the Depression. Her practicality is what gives her dignity; as she cares for Laura we realize how much Amanda herself needs to be cared for. Her refusal to give in to her nostalgia, even while she indulges in it, enhances her character and makes us susceptible to her longing.

Tom is smothered by such a woman. He fights with her, in part, because she continually tells him what to do: how to eat; how to sleep; how to get ahead. But he fights, also, because her standards represent the conventionality of family responsibility:

AMANDA: Where are you going?
TOM: I'm going to the *movies!*
AMANDA: I don't believe that lie!

[Tom crouches toward her, overtowering her tiny figure. She

backs away, gasping.]

TOM: I'm going to opium dens! Yes, opium dens, dens of vice and criminals, hang-outs, Mother. I've joined the Hogan Gang, I'm a hired assassin, I carry a tommy-gun in a violin case! I run a string of cat-houses in the Valley! They call me Killer, Killer Wingfield, I'm leading a double-life, a simple, honest warehouse worker by day, by night a dynamic *czar* of the *underworld, Mother.* I go to gambling casinos, I spin away fortunes on the roulette table! I wear a patch over one eye and a false mustache, sometimes I put on green whiskers. On those occasions they call me—*El Diablo!* Oh, I could tell you things to make you sleepless! My enemies plan to dynamite this place. They're going to blow us all sky-high some night! I'll be glad, very happy, and so will you! You'll go up, on a broomstick, over Blue Mountain with seventeen gentlemen callers! You ugly—babbling old—*witch.*

He can no more accept her memories of genteel home life in Blue Mountain than he can the spirit with which she has managed to carry on. Both suffocate him. The dead family world of the past is as stultifying as the present. Tom feels the need to escape both:

You know it don't take much intelligence to get yourself into a nailed-up coffin, Laura. But who in hell ever got himself out of one without removing one nail?

[As if in answer, the father's grinning photograph lights up. The scene dims out.]

The absent father, who still represents the memory of romantic family love to Amanda, is the possibility of romantic escape from family to Tom. He loves his sister Laura, yet he will not accept the responsibility for her which Amanda demands of him. The Wingfields are only a ghost of the family of security, but even this demand to be close-knit repels the restless Tom.

TOM'S LOVE FOR LAURA

Tom's love for Laura needs to be emphasized, I think, not only because it is one part of the final image of the play—the moment of revelation toward which the action tends—but because it shows Williams's interest in the special qualities of those whom the world has hurt. They are the delicate and fragile people, too sensitive to be able to withstand the crude and harsh necessities by which life drives us along. They have an extraordinary awareness of hidden, almost mystical, qualities of spiritual beauty; and this openness dooms them to be crushed or perverted by the animal vigor of the world.

Laura's specialness is seen largely in contrast with Jim, her gentleman caller. He is, by all odds, the kindest of Williams's emissaries from reality, perhaps because his faith in the American dream of self-improvement and success is so complete as to be itself a touching illusion:

> JIM *[Going after him]:* You know, Shakespeare—I'm going to sell you a bill of goods!
>
> TOM: What goods?
>
> JIM: A course I'm taking.
>
> TOM: Huh?
>
> JIM: In public speaking! You and me, we're not the warehouse type.
>
> TOM: Thanks—that's good news. But what has public speaking got to do with it?
>
> JIM: It fits you for—executive positions!
>
> TOM: Awww.
>
> JIM: I tell you it's done a helluva lot for me.
>
> *[Image on screen: Executive at his desk.]*

Williams mocks Jim just enough in the use of the slide projection so that we need not take him seriously, yet he makes Jim's naïveté spring from high spirits and an openheartedness which is endearing. He is healthy, happy, and full of hope, but set next to Laura and her needs he is crude, clumsy, and shallow:

> You know what I judge to be the trouble with you? Inferiority complex! Know what that is? That's what they call it when someone low-rates himself!

So much for the intricacies of the human personality. To Jim, Laura's problems are easily solved and he sets about, in his well-intentioned way, to cure her. First, he persuades her to dance; and then, caught up himself in the romance of the moment, he kisses her. But Laura needs more than a kiss, more in fact than Jim could ever give her. She needs a tenderness and love that she will never find. Her needs are so great that to satisfy them would mean altering the real world to fit her, changing it into a world like that inhabited by her glass animals, full of delicacy, beauty, and tender harmony.

When this incompatible couple waltzes into the glass menagerie, they begin to destroy it. At first, Laura does not mind. She is too thrilled with the prospect of being normal to care whether her glass unicorn has lost its distinctive horn. But the accident warns us of what Jim awkwardly confesses after the kiss—that he has made a mistake and will see her no more:

> I wish that you would—say something.
>
> *[She bites her lip which was trembling and then bravely smiles. She opens her hand again on the broken glass ornament. Then she gently takes his hand and raises it level with her own. She carefully places the unicorn in the palm of his hand, then pushes his fingers closed upon it.]*
>
> What are you—doing that for? You want me to have him?— Laura?
>
> *[She nods.]*
>
> What for?
>
> LAURA: A—souvenir.

Laura now knows that she belongs to a different world from Jim. He wandered into a zoo of exotic animals, but that was on his day off and he must return to the workaday world.

THE GLASS MENAGERIE AS A SEMIAUTOBIOGRAPHICAL PLAY

In an article in the New York Times, *Williams tells critic Robert Van Gelder that* The Glass Menagerie *is semiautobiographical, reflecting the playwright's family life in St. Louis.*

The Glass Menagerie is "semi-autobiographical—that is, it is based on the conditions of my life in St. Louis. The apartment where we lived wasn't as dingy and poverty-stricken as that in the play, but I can't say much for it, even so. It was a rented, furnished apartment, all over-stuffed furniture, and the only nice room in it was my sister's room. That room was painted white and she had put up a lot of shelves and filled them with little glass animals. When I'd come home from the shoe place where I worked—my father owned it, I hated it—I would go in and sit in her room. She was the member of the family with whom I was most in sympathy and, looking back, her glass menagerie had a meaning for me. Nostalgia helped—it makes the little flat in the play more attractive really than our apartment was—and as I thought about it the glass animals came to represent the fragile, delicate ties that must be broken, that you inevitably break, when you try to fulfill yourself."

There will be no normal love of marriage and family for Laura nor for any of the Wingfields. Laura is too tender, too special, too fragile like her glass menagerie. It is Tom's painful sensitivity to Laura's predicament which makes him love her and which drives him from her. But he cannot escape Laura. The necessity of leaving her and the guilt over doing so, haunt him:

> Oh, Laura, Laura, I tried to leave you behind me, but I am more faithful than I intended to be! I reach for a cigarette, I cross the street, I run into the movies or a bar, I buy a drink, I speak to the nearest stranger—anything that can blow your candles out!

> *[Laura bends over the candles.]*

> For nowadays the world is lit by lightning! Blow out your candles, Laura—and so good-bye....

> *[She blows the candles out.]*

Laura's painful encounter with the world's lightning represents all of the Wingfields. Amanda's last glance at her husband's picture reveals as much of her as does Tom's final speech of him. The family is the supreme case of love trying to struggle against the world, and the family fails. Fundamentally romantic, Williams evokes the beauty of failure, the beauty which must fail.

WILLIAMS'S SENSITIVITY FOR THE FAMILY

While family life is impossibly difficult, Williams does not actually reject it. Instead, he allows his characters—and his audience—the full "pleasures" of family nostalgia and suffering. It is Williams's peculiar ability to do so without bathos. We can savor the situation because, like Amanda, we are never lost in it uninterruptedly. Williams insures his family memories against outright sentimentality by a delightful (and convenient) comic touch. He does not really create a comic perspective, which would change the meaning of his vision and would suggest the sanity of compromise. Rather, he edges the serious matter of his plays with humor. For example, early in *Orpheus Descending* one of the minor characters declares that most people find hate in marriage and an outlet in money. Her laughter at this observation is a perfect Williams moment. It conveys his temporary emotional defense against the painful truth. *Streetcar* is framed in the same way, with a dirty joke at the beginning and an ironic double entendre at the end: "This game is seven-card stud." Williams seldom maintains his comic view, however, since it is for him, and for his strongest characters, a temporary way of keeping the world at bay. When he waxes "true," his characters speak directly, often lyrically, and the ironic edge disappears. Maggie, in *Cat,* has this edge, this style as part of her character. For her, it is a defense against the suffocating world of her in-laws. At private moments she may drop this defense; the curtain parts, and we see the loneliness, the isolation, and the gentleness within her. The painful inner lives of his characters remain as desperate as ever, only we are given alternate moments of rest from the hurt.

The distancing in *The Glass Menagerie* is fully and artfully done. In Tom's opening speech, for example, the touch of social comment which appears mocks the world of the middle class as well as itself:

> In Spain there was revolution. Here there was only shouting and confusion. . . . This is the social background of the play.

Later, when this motif reappears, it is directly associated with the dilemmas of the Wingfield family. Their private world looks out on the social world in the same way that their windows look out on the alley. Tom says to the audience:

> Couples would come outside, to the relative privacy of the alley. You could see them kissing behind ash-pits and telephone poles. This was the compensation for lives that passed like mine, without any change or adventure. . . .
>
> In Spain there was Guernica!

And immediately Amanda unwittingly provides the mocking counterpoint:

> A fire-escape landing's a poor excuse for a porch. *[She spreads a newspaper on a step and sits down, gracefully and demurely as if she were settling into a swing on a Mississippi veranda.]* What are you looking at?

. . . Williams tries to have his sentiment and mock it, too, using these devices both to intensify the family drama and to pull back from it. These "plastic" elements, then, are Williams's way of using the realistic situation while not being exclusively bound to it. The core of the play is the attempt by Amanda to find a family and the desire by Tom to escape from family. This surface action is alternately heightened and diminished by these nonrealistic devices. We are asked to embrace the characters and to laugh at them, to empathize and then to sympathize. Much of the same strategy can be seen in the dialogue, once we are alerted to it. Amanda's telephone campaign to sell subscriptions to the magazine *Companion* is filled with this juxtaposition of tears and laughter. More poignantly, her memories of her home life in Blue Mountain are made up of a dramatic alternation between vivid nostalgia and shrewd practicality:

> Finally there were no more vases to hold them, every available space was filled with jonquils. No vases to hold them? All right, I'll hold them myself! And then I—*[She stops in front of the picture. Music plays.]* met your father! Malaria fever and jonquils and then—this—boy.... *[She switches on the rose-colored lamp.]*
>
> I hope they get here before it starts to rain.

Nearly lost in the intensity of her memory, Amanda begins to speak as though the past were the present, only to be brought up short by the reality of her situation. The rose-colored lamp is both a reprise of her vulnerability to charm and an instance of her coping, in the only way she knows how, with the situation in which that vulnerability has placed her: she puts a good light on harsh truths, and she dresses up the faded room to catch the gentleman caller for sister. And one might even say that all the Wingfields get caught out in the rain, away from the warm safety of home. Thus, the drama is embodied in the rhetoric and through its sequential movement each emotionally resonant element is followed by a flat deflation.

FAMILY BATTLES

Williams uses a similar technique to add a more complex texture to the raw emotions of the Wingfields' family battles. Tom's angry speech denouncing his mother as a witch is slightly muted by his satiric, fanciful tone. But if the direct emotion is reduced in volume, it can also be said that the sense of calculation which Tom's imagery implies makes the hurt Amanda receives all the keener for having been so carefully designed. And in the rare moments when mother and son can talk to, rather than at, each other, Williams manages this shift in tone with greatest delicacy:

> AMANDA: When I was a girl in Blue Mountain and it was suspected that a young man drank, the girl whose attentions he had been receiving, if any girl *was*, would sometimes speak to the minister of his church, or rather her father would if her

father was living, and sort of feel him out on the young man's character. That is the way such things are discreetly handled to keep a young woman from making a tragic mistake!

TOM: Then how did you happen to make a tragic mistake?

AMANDA: That innocent look of your father's had everyone fooled! He *smiled*—the world was *enchanted!* No girl can do worse than put herself at the mercy of a handsome appearance! I hope that Mr. O'Connor is not too good-looking.

TOM: No, he's not too good-looking. He's covered with freckles and hasn't too much of a nose.

AMANDA: He's not right-down homely, though?

TOM: Not right-down homely. Just medium homely, I'd say.

The lines play first between Amanda's nostalgia and Tom's blunt irony, and then between her ecstatic memories (with the painful lesson they teach) and Tom's more gentle teasing. At moments such as these, the play's tone becomes a mode of encounter between characters, its surface ingenuity a way of revealing inner lives. The Wingfields exist most vividly when they appear to us caught between moments of direct revelation of their psyches and moments of indirect relief from that painful confrontation. In *The Glass Menagerie* the longing for the family of security is mocked but never abandoned, indulged even as it is shown up.

The Outsider in
The Glass Menagerie

Gerald Weales

Gerald Weales contends that the major characters in
The Glass Menagerie are outsiders, individuals who
are unable or unwilling either to cope with or conform to a dull and cruel world. Weales argues that the
outsider characters found in the Wingfield family are
character types that populate subsequent plays by
Williams. Tom is an outsider because of his poetic nature. In contrast with Jim, who seeks success naively
in a conventional world, Tom is a fugitive who wants
to escape conformity. Tom's nonconformity is represented by his poetic temperament, his sensitivity, and
his general cultural and artistic predisposition.

Weales suggests that Laura's character also reappears as
an outsider throughout Williams's work. His major plays
have female characters like Laura who are physically fragile and emotionally terrified to face a harsh and frightening
world. Amanda is also a prototype for Williams's faded aristocrat, haunted by poverty and frustration, who looks back
on better days, real or imagined. Both Laura and Amanda
display the physical or mental sickness that often marks
the outsider as one who is unable to face the demands of
reality: Laura has a limp and Amanda is prone to paranoia.

Gerald Weales has taught graduate and undergraduate
drama classes at the University of Pennsylvania, Philadel-
phia. His articles on drama have appeared in *Drama Sur-
vey, Tulane Drama Review,* and *Antioch Review.* Weales is
the author of *Religion in Modern English Drama.*

All of Williams' protagonists and many of his subsidiary
characters are outsiders, unable or unwilling to conform to
the dull or cruel world in which they find themselves. Cora
and Billy, the slut and the homosexual who join forces in the

From *American Drama Since World War II* by Gerald Weales (New York: Harcourt,
Brace & World, 1962). Copyright ©1962 by Gerald Weales. Reprinted by permission of
the author.

short story, "Two on a Party," are militant examples:

> It was a rare sort of moral anarchy, doubtless, that held them
> together, a really fearful shared hatred of everything that was
> restrictive and which they felt to be false in the society they
> lived in and against the grain of which they continually oper-
> ated. They did not dislike what they called "squares." They
> loathed and despised them, and for the best of reasons. Their
> existence was a never-ending contest with the squares of the
> world, the squares who have such a virulent rage at every-
> thing not in their book.

The generic name for these characters in Williams is "the
fugitive kind," a phrase that turns up first as the title of his
second full-length play, which was never published. The use
of the words in the story "One Arm" is specifically homosexual. By the time Carol Cutrere adopts the phrase in *Orpheus Descending,* as she takes Val's snakeskin jacket, a
token by which "the fugitive kind can always follow their
kind," the label belongs to the outsider who seeks the freedom that Val describes metaphorically when he tells Lady
about the legless bird that lives all his life on the wing. The
movie version of *Orpheus Descending,* of course, became *The
Fugitive Kind.*

To go to the stories for a definition of the Williams outsider is to do his protagonists a disservice; the short fiction
is redolent with a kind of lip-smacking perversity, lingers
lovingly over the details of the trade, to use a "trade" term.
In the plays, the preoccupation is not so narrow. The leading
characters are different from (implicitly, superior to) their
neighbors, but there is variety in the differences. The one
thing that all of them seem to have in common is the combination of sensitivity and imagination with corruption—
physical, spiritual, sexual disability. From the beginning, the
plays have suggested that the heroes are abnormal and that
there is something vaguely damnable about normality.

THE CONTRAST OF JIM AND TOM

Tom in *The Glass Menagerie* describes Jim, the gentleman
caller, as "an emissary from a world of reality that we were
somehow set apart from." Neither Tom, who is in some ways
Williams himself, nor his creator, who calls Jim a "nice, ordinary, young man," seems aware that the gentleman caller
is a much more important symbol than the pretentious "long
delayed but always expected something that we live for."
Jim, much more than the romantic Tom, is a condemnation

of the world Tom wants to escape from; he is an Arthur Miller character, dead wrong and almost certain, expecting optimistically that he will find success just beyond the next correspondence course. Although Williams has given him space to operate in, lines enough to be damning in their glibness and pathetic in their naïveté, it is apparent here and later that Williams cannot really come to care seriously about the Jims who try to operate in the real world. He is more concerned with those who reject or are rejected by it. The three Wingfields are Williams' kind although only Tom becomes a fugitive. Tom is supposed to be a poet, a spirit too free for the confines of the warehouse that encloses him; before the play is over, no longer able to find escape at the movies, he leaves his family "attempting to find in motion what was lost in space." That is, he joins the merchant marine. His sister Laura is a painfully shy girl with a slight limp, a physical and emotional cripple, who takes refuge in her glass collection and in the old records that belonged to their father, who deserted the family years before the curtain rises. Amanda, the mother, the strongest character in the play, has one foot in reality in her struggle to hold the family together and the other in the illusionary world of her girlhood, the genteel tag end of the aristocratic South. Her past, the play suggests, may be as imaginary as its application to her present, for there is never any evidence that Amanda's memories are real ones. Amanda and Laura are defeated by the world, fade at the end of the play into an amorphous future, all scrim and lighting effects; Tom survives to tell the story, but he is fated to be a stranger in the world. Among them, the three Wingfields manage to display most of the characteristics of the later Williams characters.

Both Laura and Tom have the sensitivity; with Laura it is allied to physical fragility and virginal withdrawal, with Tom it is part of his poetic temperament. Other Lauras turn up in Matilda in *You Touched Me!,* Alma in *Summer and Smoke,* and Isabel in *Period of Adjustment.* Brick in *Cat on a Hot Tin Roof* is also a kind of Laura; Williams even gives him a broken ankle, like Laura's limp, to serve as a visual symbol of his "moral paralysis." Most of the heroines, whether they are Laura's type or not, have their glass menageries, which, like Amanda's Blue Mountain memories, keep them from seeing the ugliness of a frightening world. Blanche has the mythical Shep Huntleigh as a potential gentleman caller and she acquires a Chinese lantern to put over the naked bulb in the Kowalski apartment. Matilda has the silver to polish; Serafina, in *The Rose Tattoo,* her urn of ashes; Lady, in *Orpheus,* the simulation in her confectionery of her dead father's wine garden; Alexandra, in *Sweet Bird,* her hashish and her oxygen.

TOM'S POETIC TEMPERAMENT

Tom's poetic temperament turns up again and again in the later plays and, for the most part, it is as ambiguously presented as it is in *The Glass Menagerie.* All that we really know about Tom as an artist is that he jots verses down on the lids of boxes in the warehouse where he works, and that Williams did the same thing when he worked in a warehouse in his youth. It may be that Tom, like the young man in [Eugene O'Neill's] *Long Day's Journey into Night,* has the habit of the poet without the makings. For Williams, that does not seem to matter. Sensitivity is implicit in the character who, like Billy in "Two on a Party," manages to be "a sort of artist *manqué"* and has "a touch of homesickness for what that was." His pseudo-artistic characters aside, Williams seems to have only a flaccid idea of what art is. He describes the interior set of *The Glass Menagerie* as "dim and poetic" and, fifteen years later, suggests that a cyclorama be used in *Sweet Bird* to achieve "a poetic unity of mood"; a good many of his general comments on writing that fall between the two stage directions display the same fondness for the vague. Williams uses the word *poetic* as loosely and as enthusiastically as Blanche might; so it is hardly surprising that his characters need only cultural and artistic pretensions, not achievements, to indicate their differentness from the people around them. Thus, Blanche can display the high-school teacher's name-dropping familiarity with literary figures ("Only Poe! Only Mr. Edgar Allan Poe!—could do it justice!") and Alma can take part in the meeting of a literary club, which Williams presents satirically, without either of them losing her standing among the Williams near artists. Both Mrs. Stone, of the spring in Rome, and Alexandra in *Sweet Bird* are ex-actresses, and even though their success depended more on their beauty than their artistry, they belong to Tom Wingfield's fraternity. So, too, does Vee Talbot, the primitive painter of *Orpheus Descending,* even though (or because) her painting is the objectivization of her sexual frustration. The most preposterous of the Williams artists are Sebastian, the poet of *Suddenly Last Summer,* and Val Xavier, the Orpheus who does the descending. The first may well be intended satirically—at least I cannot take seriously the poet who produces one poem a year, each time after a nine-month gestation period—but Val, I am afraid, is serious. In *Battle of Angels,* the embryonic version of *Orpheus,* Val is, incredibly, writing *the book;* in *Orpheus,* Williams wisely takes away his pen and hands him a guitar, which not only better suits his mythic origins, but which can be worked less portentously into the action of the play. Even so, Val insists on calling the instrument his "life's companion," fondles it so lovingly that he ends by suggesting Christopher Fry's charming Chaplain in *The Lady's Not for Burning,* who calls his violin "my better half . . . my mistress . . . my angel." The only dead-certain poet in the body of Williams' plays is Byron, who turns up in *Camino Real,* but it is his manner and not his matter that gets him into that play.

AMANDA AS THE FADED ARISTOCRAT

Just as Laura the recluse and Tom the poet turn up in other plays, bearing other names and faces, so too does Amanda the faded aristocrat. The short plays and stories are loaded with serious or comic, New Orleans or deep South, versions of the Amanda character—*The Lady of Larkspur Lotion,* Miss Collins in *Portrait of a Madonna,* Mme. Duvenet in *Auto-Da-Fé,* the two ladies in *Lord Byron's Love Letter,* Cornelia Scott in *Something Unspoken,* Miss Jelkes in "The Night of the Iguana." All of them must be hounded in some way—by poverty, by age, by frustration—and all of them must look back fondly on better days, either real or fictional. Blanche in *Streetcar* is certainly the most famous of the Williams faded ladies. Much of her manner—her pretense at gentility, the affectations of her speech, her verbal withdrawal from Stanley—goes back to an imaginary Belle Reve, one that existed, if it existed at all, in the years before Blanche was around to know it; the Belle Reve she describes, the plantation Stella escaped from, was a place of slow death and decay ("Crumble and fade and—regrets—recriminations"). Blanche, more than she knows, is a product of Belle Reve, true descendant of those "improvident grand fathers and fathers and uncles and brothers" who "exchanged the land for their epic fornications." When *Streetcar* first appeared in 1947, we were still within shouting distance of those days when critics thought of plays always in social terms; it was not surprising that Blanche became a symbol of the Old South, that romantic invention of Southern ladies and Northern historians, whose cultural and human virtues were doomed to destruction in the face of the vitality and vulgarity of the New South—Stanley. Although Williams' plays have, from the beginning, often contained specific social criticism, his attachment to the Blanches is more than a search for a social symbol. Her corruption is as important to him as her sensitivity; both characteristics make her an uncomfortable visitor in a middle-class world. He consistently uses the shell of the Southern aristocracy for the double value it gives him. This is made quite clear in "The Night of the Iguana" in which he describes Miss Jelkes's "historical Southern family of great but now moribund vitality": "There had been an efflorescence among them of nervous talents and sickness, of drunkards and poets, gifted artists and sexual degenerates, together with fanatically proper and squeamish old ladies of both sexes." The sentence reads like a cast list for a Williams play. Sandra in *Battle of Angels* makes the same point when she describes herself as rotten and neurotic, but identifies with Val, "You—savage. And me—aristocrat. Both of us things whose license has been revoked in the civilized world. Both of us equally damned and for the same good reason. Because we both want freedom." This kind of leaden explicitness disappears in the rewrite, in *Orpheus Descending,* in which Sandra has become Carol Cutrere, but Carol's actions and many of her lines still say the same thing.

The once elegant Mrs. Venable in *Suddenly Last Summer* is a variation on the type. Her connections are not with a historical past, but with a personal one. She is one of the ex-beauties, like Mrs. Stone and Alexandra Del Lago and Camille as she appears in *Camino Real,* although—unlike the other ladies—she is not feeding (nor can she) the illusion of youth by buying love. Chance Wayne is a male version of the aging women and so, too, is Brick, although the ex-athlete in him brings him closer to the ex-actress in Alexandra than to the ex-beauty.

Two other important identification marks for the Williams outsiders are their physical and mental sicknesses and their preoccupation with sex. The first of these is apparent in *The Glass Menagerie* in Laura's limp and in the description of

Amanda as "not paranoic, but her life is paranoia." Blanche is specifically identified as a "neurasthenic personality." Alma has to have her tablets ("The prescription number is 96814. I think of it as the telephone number of God!"), and Lady, Alexandra, Chance, Sebastian, Isabel Haverstick are all pilleaters, too. Kilroy in *Camino Real* has a weak heart; Brick, a broken ankle; Big Daddy, cancer. Mrs. Venable has had a stroke, but in *Suddenly Last Summer* that is hardly noticeable, for in that play Williams' fondness for medical mumbo jumbo runs rampant; not only is Catharine threatened with a lobotomy, she is given a truth injection on stage and the audience is offered a parody paradigm of the scientific process as solemn as that of the mad scientist in old horror films. It is obvious that the mental and physical diseases, real and imagined, that afflict the characters are partly symbolic; all of them, like Laura, are crippled in the face of a world that is cruel and demanding.

CHAPTER 3

Structure, Influences, and Criticism of *The Glass Menagerie*

READINGS ON
THE GLASS MENAGERIE

Symbolism and Imagery in *The Glass Menagerie*

Roger B. Stein

Roger Stein discusses the symbolism and imagery
that Williams uses to unify *The Glass Menagerie*. The
most obvious organizing symbol is the glass menagerie itself, which Stein says represents Laura's fragile
world, her search for beauty, and her life of illusion.
Stein explains that Williams deepens the plight of the
characters by setting their lives against both a social
and spiritual catastrophe. The time of the play is
1939, following a decade of exhausting economic
crisis and facing the threat of world war. Against
this backdrop the characters are engulfed in a larger
social tragedy wherein success and the American
Dream are not to be found. Stein also discusses
Williams's use of Christian symbolism to define the
characters and their situation. Like the social setting,
the spiritual environment is bleak. At the end of the
play, the audience realizes that all of the characters
end up in the dark, both literally with the power failure and personally with a spiritual emptiness.

Roger B. Stein is on the faculty of the McIntyre
Department of Art at the University of Virginia in
Charlottesville. He is the author of numerous works,
including *American Imagination, John Ruskin and
Aesthetic Thought in America,* and *Susquehanna: Im-
ages of a Settled Landscape.*

The Glass Menagerie (1945) was Tennessee Williams' first
major theatrical success. Over the years he has written
much, some of high quality indeed, but nothing better than
this play which established him as an important post-war
playwright. "The dramatist of frustration," John Gassner

From "*The Glass Menagerie* Revisited: Catastrophe Without Violence," by Roger B.
Stein, *Western Humanities Review*, vol. 18 (Spring 1964), 141–53. Copyright ©1964 by
Western Humanities Review. Reprinted by permission of *Western Humanities Review*.

dubbed him in 1948 after *Streetcar,* but unlike most of his later plays, *The Glass Menagerie* projects not a series of violent confrontations leading to catastrophe but a vision of lonely human beings who fail to make contact, who are isolated from each other and from society, and who seem ultimately abandoned in the universe.

What holds the play together are Tom's remembrances of things past, not plot or characterization. Tom, the poet-narrator and author's surrogate, called "Shakespeare" in the warehouse, organizes the drama symbolically through language and image. This is the "new plastic theatre" of which Williams spoke in his production notes, a revelation not through dramatic struggle but through the allusive power of the word, the accretion of symbolic clusters which bear the meaning, reinforced dramaturgically through lighting, music, the distancing devices of a narrator and, as originally planned, of screen images.

SYMBOLISM IN THE PLAY

The glass menagerie is itself the most obvious organizing symbol. It embodies the fragility of Laura's world, her search for beauty; it registers sensitively changes in lighting and stands in vivid contrast to the harshness of the outer world which can (and does) shatter it so easily. The unicorn can become the gift to Jim the Gentleman Caller, whose anticipation and appearance form the plot of the play, only when it has lost its mythical uniqueness, the horn, when dream becomes momentarily possibility before it is obliterated at the end. The magic of Prince Charming's kiss can not work ("Stumblejohn," he brands himself in the published version of the play, taking on for the moment Laura's crippled condition). The "little silver slipper of a moon" on which Amanda has asked Laura to wish becomes an ironic image of Laura's isolated condition, but Amanda, wrapped up in her own illusion and selling magazine subscriptions and brassieres (like the "Gay Deceivers" with which she tries to stuff Laura before Jim appears) prefers to believe not in Tom's favorite D.H. Lawrence, but in Cinderella and courtly love and *Gone with the Wind,* the novel to which she compares Bessie May Harper's latest effort in *The Homemaker's Companion.* The ironies of the allusive imagery proliferate: Amanda's heroic efforts as homemaker are unsuccessful (the father appears only as a happy doughboy photographic image), and Margaret Mitchell's depression romance about the desirable Scarlett O'Hara in a lost Eden, a South fantasized in the national imagination during the Depression, only makes Laura look more forlorn. Finally one may note that the title image itself of *Gone with the Wind* underlines the evanescent quality of this dream and all of the Wingfields' illusions. As such, it points directly to the last line of the play and Tom's injunction to "Blow out your candles, Laura."

On the level of plot, this widening circle of reference enhances the credibility of the dramatic situation. Given Amanda's sham version of idealized love and a fantasy past, how could the Gentleman Caller's visit be other than a failure? Despite Amanda's dress which is "historical almost," despite the attempt to live in the nineteenth century when the electric power goes off, Jim is not Rhett Butler but an "emissary from a world of reality," as Tom calls him, an engaged twentieth-century man on vacation. The flickering candlelight of Jim's scene with Laura is not enough to sustain the illusion; at the end of their scene this illusion collapses and we are left in darkness.

THE PLAY'S SOCIAL BACKDROP

But *The Glass Menagerie* is built upon more than the poignant plot of illusion and frustration in the lives of little people. Williams has deepened the losses of individuals by pointing to social and even spiritual catastrophe. The time of the play is 1939, as the narrative frame makes explicit both at the beginning and the end. The life of illusion is not confined to the Wingfields alone. As Tom says, "the huge middle class of America was matriculating in a school for the blind." What he calls the "social background" of the play has an important role. The international backdrop is Guernica and the song America sings is "The World Is Waiting for the Sunrise," for the sober truth is that America is still in the Depression and on the brink of war. The note of social disaster runs throughout the drama, fixing the lives of individuals against the larger canvas.

Amanda's anxieties are in large part economic and there is money behind many of her illusions: her mythical suitors were all wealthy men, as are her magazine heroes; she computes the money Tom would save by giving up smoking. When Tom complains of the grimness of life in the shoe factory, she replies, "Try and you will SUCCEED!" If this is another of Amanda's illusions, it is one shared by her fellow Americans, for "try and you will succeed" is the traditional motto of the American dream of success, the theme of confident self-reliance canonized in the romances of Horatio Alger.

JIM AND THE AMERICAN DREAM

It is not Amanda, however, but Jim, the emissary from reality, who is the chief spokesman for the American dream. To Jim the warehouse is not a prison but a rung on the ladder toward success. He believes in self-improvement through education, and the lecture on self-confidence which he reads to Laura is part of the equipment of the future executive. He is awed by the fortune made in chewing gum and rhapsodizes on the theme of the future material progress of America: "All that remains is for the industry to get itself under way! Full steam—*Knowledge—Zzzzzp! Money—Zzzzzp! Power!* That's the cycle democracy is built on!"

Yet when the theme of success is superimposed upon the lives of the characters, the social irony emerges. Father was not the successful businessman, but a telephone man who "fell in love with long distances." Tom, the substitute father, refuses to pay the light bill, plunges his family into darkness, and then runs out, and Amanda sells subscriptions and brassieres only at the loss of her dignity. Jim's own dream of success seems to have reached its peak in high school. (Williams later explored this theme more fully in *Cat on a Hot Tin Roof.*) The trek upward through the depression years is disappointing, but the indomitable optimist is not discouraged.

The experience of the 1930s did not turn Williams into a proletarian writer or social realist, but it did open up for him a darker vision of American life which he suggests to his audience but which is denied to his characters, still "matriculating in a school for the blind": a belief that the American dream is itself a sham and a failure. In his essay "The Catastrophe of Success," Williams said that "the Cinderella story is our favorite national myth, the cornerstone of the film industry if not of the Democracy itself." The social catastrophe inherent in *The Glass Menagerie* lies precisely in the fact that Laura is *not* Cinderella: the silver slipper does not finally fit, and Jim is not Prince Charming but one of the innumerable Americans who would soon be moving overseas in troop ships. As Tom says at the end, "for nowadays the world is lit

by lightning! Blow out your candles, Laura—and so good-
bye. . . ." The world which had been waiting for the sunrise
burst with bombardments instead, and the lives of the Wingfields at the end are absorbed in the larger social tragedy.

Christian Imagery in the Play

Williams goes even further than this, however. The end of the
play involves more than just the snuffing out of Laura's
hope; it is even more than social tragedy. It is a *Götterdäm-
merung* [catastrophic collapse]. For the candles and the lightning which close the play have appeared together before. We
are told by Amanda that the candelabrum "used to be on the
altar at the church of the Heavenly Rest. It was melted a little out of shape when the church burnt down. Lightning
struck it one spring." Amanda's comment opens up another
dimension of the drama, and reminds us that Williams, in-
heritor of a Southern religious tradition which includes writers like Faulkner and Robert Penn Warren, has persistently
drawn upon the language of Christian symbolism to define
his characters' human situations. Amanda's quiet comment
is a far cry from the hysterical ravings of the defrocked Reverend T. Lawrence Shannon in *Night of the Iguana* about
wanting "to go back to the church and preach the gospel of
God as Lightning and Thunder." The pervasive religious
overtones of *The Glass Menagerie* never obscure the literal
line of the story or seem self-conscious, as they frequently do
in the later plays. Ultimately they try to locate the catastrophe at the end beyond human pathos and social tragedy.

Williams' stage directions clearly indicate his intention.
The lighting for Laura should resemble that "used in early
religious portraits of female saints or madonnas." The scene
where Tom tells his mother that a Gentleman Caller will appear Williams entitles "Annunciation." The dressing of
Laura for the Caller's appearance should be "devout and ritualistic." During her scene with Jim she is lit "inwardly with
altar candles," and when Jim withdraws after kissing her
Williams informs us that the "holy candles in the altar of
Laura's face have been snuffed out. There is a look of almost
infinite desolation."

Those overtones extend beyond Williams' hints to the director and become part of the fabric of dramatic action. The
first scene in both the acting version and the library edition
of the play opens on this note. In the former, Amanda nar-

rates her "funny experience" of being denied a seat in the Episcopal church because she has not rented a pew. The idea of the Wingfields' exclusion from Christian ceremony is established thus at the outset, and it is underlined by the ensuing talk of digesting food, mastication, and salivary glands. In the Wingfield apartment, eating is an animal process only; it lacks ritual significance. The library edition opens with Amanda's call to Tom, "We can't say grace until you come to the table," and then moves on to the question of digestion. The lines are different, but their import is the same. When the Gentleman Caller comes, the scene is repeated, only this time it is Laura whose absence holds up "grace."

Amanda, who condemns instinct and urges Tom to think in terms of the mind and spirit, as "Christian adults" do, is often characterized in Christian terms. Her music, in the library edition, is "Ave Maria." As a girl she could only cook angel food cake. She urges Laura, "Possess your soul in patience," and then speaks of her dress for the dinner scene as "resurrected" from a trunk. Her constant refrain to Tom is "Rise an' Shine," and she sells subscriptions to her friends by waking them early in the morning and then sympathizing with them as "Christian martyrs." Laura is afraid to tell her mother she has left the business school because "when you're disappointed, you get that awful suffering look on your face, like the picture of Jesus' mother in the museum!"

The next picture Laura mentions is the one of Jim in the yearbook. Though the context seems secular enough at this point—Jim is a high school hero—his religious function emerges later on. In the "Annunciation" scene, when Amanda learns that the Gentleman Caller's name is O'Connor, she says, "that, of course, means fish—tomorrow is Friday!" The remark functions not only literally, since Jim is Irish Catholic, but also figuratively, for the fish is the traditional symbol of Christ. In a very real sense both Amanda and Laura are searching for a Savior who will come to help them, to save them, to give their drab lives meaning.

Tom is unable to play this role himself. Though he appears as the angel of the Annunciation, he denies the world of belief and in a bitter speech to his mother calls himself "El Diablo." With him Christian terms appear only as imprecations: "what in Christ's name" or "that God damn Rise and Shine." When Tom returns home drunk one night, he tells Laura of a stage show he has seen which is shot through with Christian symbolism, none of which he perceives. Here the magician, Malvolio, whose name suggests bad will, dislike, or even hate, plays the role of the modern Christ. He performs the miracle of turning water into wine and then goes on to blasphemy by turning the wine into beer and then whiskey. He also produces his proper symbol, the fish, but it is gold-fish, as if stained by modern materialism. Most important, he escapes from a nailed coffin. But Tom reads the symbolism of this trick in personal terms only. When Laura tries to keep him from awakening Amanda, Tom retorts:

> Goody, goody! Pay 'er back for all those "Rise an' Shines." You know it don't take much intelligence to get yourself into a nailed-up coffin, Laura. But who in hell ever got himself out of one without removing one nail?

The illumination of the father's photograph at this point suggests one answer to this question, but the pattern of Christian imagery in the drama, especially when reinforced here by the "Rise an' Shine" refrain, should suggest to us another answer—the resurrection itself—which Tom's rejection of Christian belief prevents him from seeing.

It remains therefore for Jim to come as the Savior to this Friday night supper. The air of expectancy is great, with the ritualistic dressing of Laura, the tension, and the oppressive heat. Jim's arrival is marked by the coming of rain, but the hopes of fertility and renewal which this might suggest are soon dashed. Laura's attempt to come to the dinner table is a failure, signaled by a clap of thunder, and Tom's muttered grace, "For these and all thy mercies, God's Holy Name be praised," is bitterly ironic, mocked by what follows. The only paradise within reach is Paradise Dance Hall, with its "Waste Land" mood of slow and sensuous rhythms and couples kissing behind ashpits and telephone poles, "the compensation for lives that passed . . . without any change or adventure," as Tom remarks. The failure of electric power after dinner—previsioning the blackout of the world—leads to Amanda's joking question, "Where was Moses when the lights went off?" This suggests another savior who would lead his people from the desert into the promised land, but the answer to her question is "In the dark."

Jim's attempt to play the modern savior is an abysmal failure. In the after dinner scene, he offers Laura the sacrament—wine and "life-savers," in this case—and a Dale Carnegie version of the Sermon on the Mount—self-help rather than divine help—but to no avail. At the end of the play Laura and Amanda are, as the joke bitterly reminds us, "in the dark," and Tom's last lines announce the final failure, the infinite desolation: "For nowadays the world is lit by lightning. Blow out your candles, Laura—and so goodbye."

Here as elsewhere in his plays Williams draws upon his frightened characters' preference for soft candlelight to harsh daylight or electric bulbs, not only because it serves him dramaturgically to establish his conception of a new plastic theater where evanescent characters and images flicker across the stage momentarily, but also because his characters so often want to withdraw from the blinding light of reality into the softer world of illusion. At the end of *The Glass Menagerie,* however, the blackout is even more catastrophic, for it not only envelops the Laura of Tom's memory and serves as another reminder of the blackout of war which shrouds the world: it is also the denial of any final "Rise an' Shine" for these frail creatures. The church has been struck by lightning, and all hope of resurrection has been lost in this damned universe where belief turns into metaphor, where humankind seems abandoned by its God, and where the echoes of prayer are heard only in blasphemy or irony. The bleakness of Williams' vision in *The Glass Menagerie* is complete. If Tom is released finally, it is in the words of Job, "And I only am escaped alone to tell thee." It is as the author's surrogate, as writer and chronicler of catastrophe, that he emerges at the end.

Expressionism in
The Glass Menagerie

Nancy M. Tischler

In his production notes for *The Glass Menagerie*,
Tennessee Williams writes that subjectivity is closer
to the truth than photographic realism. Nancy M.
Tischler writes that this idea, which is the core of
Williams's dramatic expressionist theory, frees the
playwright to infuse his work with symbolic elements, a Williams trademark. Tischler also focuses
on Williams's expressionist use of lighting and
music, both of which enhance emotional emphasis.
The apartment and its environs are designed to
create the impression of the ugliness and uniformity
of reality, the reality that Laura strives to escape.
Even the action is expressionalistically developed
because it does not rely on incident or situation;
rather, framed through Tom's memory, it depends
on quiet revelations of ordinary truths. Unlike most
of Williams's other works, *The Glass Menagerie*
combines artistic and nonrealistic techniques to
create a poetic effect.

Nancy Tischler teaches English at Pennsylvania
University, Middletown. She is the author of *Black
Masks: Negro Characters in Modern Southern Fiction*
and the editor of *Susquehanna University Studies.*

The setting of *The Glass Menagerie* was interesting in its
symbolism and technical experimentation. Moving from the
deep South to St. Louis for his story, Williams retains the
memory of the South, as a haunting presence under the superimposed Midwestern setting. The audience, never seeing
the gracious mansion that was the scene of Amanda's girlhood, feels its remembered glory and its contrast to the
mean present. Awareness of the past is always an element in

From *Tennessee Williams: Rebellious Spirit* by Nancy M. Tischler. Copyright ©1961,
1989 by Nancy M. Tischler. Published by arrangement with Carol Publishing Group,
120 Enterprise Ave., Secaucus, New Jersey 07094.

Williams' plays. His characters live beyond the fleeting moments of the drama—back into a glowing past and shrinking from a terrifying future. For both Amanda and the later Blanche of *Streetcar,* the South forms an image of youth, love, purity, all of the ideals that have crumbled along with the mansions and the family fortunes.

WILLIAMS' THEORY OF EXPRESSIONISM

Since the setting in *Menagerie* is that of a memory play, Tennessee Williams could feel free in its staging. His theory of expressionism is propounded in the introductory production notes, which are, in fact, directly applied in the play. His concept of the "new, plastic theatre" was probably influenced by Erwin Piscator, a German director who had helped him at the New School Seminar. He suggests that in *The Glass Menagerie*'s "considerably delicate or tenuous material, atmospheric touches and subtleties of direction play a particularly important part." Williams justifies such unconventional techniques as expressionism or impressionism on the basis that their subjectivity provides a "closer approach to truth." No playwright should use such devices in an effort to avoid the "responsibility of dealing with reality, or interpreting experience." But he believes that the new drama has followed the other arts in recognizing that realism is not the key to reality.

SYMBOLISM IN THE PLAY

"The straight realistic play with its genuine frigidaire and authentic ice-cubes, its characters that speak exactly as its audience speaks," he says, "corresponds to the academic landscape and has the same virtue of photographic likeness." Then, with unique optimism regarding current artistic tastes, he continues, "Everyone should know nowadays the unimportance of the photographic in art: that truth, life, or reality is an organic thing which the poetic imagination can represent or suggest, in essence, only through transformation, through changing into other forms than those which were merely present in appearance." The philosophy expressed here is in accord with the nineteenth century romantics and their followers in this century. The expressionistic concepts propounded in this preface have proved so effective in Tennessee Williams' work that set-designers have usually chosen to use expressionistic even when realistic settings are called for in Williams' manuscripts. Williams has a poet's weakness for symbols, and this modern technique frees his hand for scattering them about the stage. Their use to reflect, emphasize, and contrast with the meanings of the actions and the words has become a trademark of the Williams play.

THE GOAL OF THE ARTIST

In Memoirs, *Williams writes that the goal of his writing is to pursue the changing, transient quality of life, a condition that the playwright felt he captured in* The Glass Menagerie.

On the Broadway opening night of *Menagerie*, the performers took bow after bow, and finally they tried to get me up on the stage. I was sitting in the fourth row, and somebody extended a hand to me and I went up on the stage. And I felt embarrassed; I don't think I felt any great sense of triumph. I think writing is continually a pursuit of a very evasive quarry, and you never quite catch it.

In the essay that accompanies one of the printed editions of *Cat on a Hot Tin Roof*, I talk very honestly about my goal in writing, what I want to do. That goal is just somehow to capture the constantly evanescent quality of existence. When I do that, then I have accomplished something, but I have done it, I think, relatively few times compared to the times I have attempted it. I don't have any sense of being a fulfilled artist. And when I was writing *Menagerie*, I did not know that I was capturing it.

The Glass Menagerie projected symbolic elements in line with Williams' newly enunciated theory. To reinforce the spoken word the author recommends the use of a screen device. A legend or image projected on the screen for the duration of the scene emphasizes the most important phrase. For example, in the scene where Jim remembers that Laura is the girl who was stricken with pleurosis, whom he mistakenly nicknamed "Blue Roses," the legend on the screen accents the peculiarity of the name, and the audience, along with Laura, is made more keenly aware that although blue is beautiful, it is wrong for roses. Eddie Dowling considered this device superfluous and omitted it from the stage production, and wisely so. Mr. Gassner also considered the screen device "redundant and rather precious." Williams is "straining for effect not knowing that his simple tale, so hauntingly self-sufficient, needs no adornments."

EXPRESSIONISTIC LIGHTING AND MUSIC

Williams' expressionist theory also leads him to another variation from strictly realistic drama. The lighting changes with the mood. The stage is as dim as the participants' lives. Shafts of light flicker onto selected areas or actors, "sometimes in contradiction to what is the apparent center." When Tom and Amanda are quarreling, the light on them is low red, while Laura stands in a pool of light of that "peculiar pristine clarity such as light used in early religious portraits of saints or madonnas." The tone, strength, and occurrence of the lights have the power of emotional emphasis. In a technique reminiscent of Chekhov's, Williams heightens the emotional truths of the scenes and the reality of the internal action through unusual external effects.

The musical accompaniment of *The Glass Menagerie* is another element of Tennessee Williams' expressionism that characterizes his dramas. The theme is a tune called "The Glass Menagerie," composed by Paul Bowles. It is "like circus music, not when you are on the grounds or in the immediate vicinity of the parade, but when you are at some distance and very likely thinking of something else. . . . It expresses the surface vivacity of life and the underlying strain of immutable and inexpressible sorrow." The music becomes Laura's symbol: of this world which is like a circus for her—heard from a safe distance; and of her retreat into a world of music as well as of glass.

THE APARTMENT SETTING

The depiction of the Wingfields' apartment also follows the dicta of expressionism. The ugly uniformity of the tenements depresses Tom and makes him frantic to escape. The place is described as "one of those vast hive-like conglomerations of cellular living-units that flower as warty growths in overcrowded urban centers of lower middle-class populations." They are, says the temporarily socially conscious author, "symptomatic of the impulse of this largest and fundamentally enslaved section of American society to avoid fluidity and differentiation and to exist and function as one interfused mass of automatism." Of the characters in the play, only Tom seems aware of this grotesque uniformity; and since the whole story takes place in his memory, he would naturally exaggerate the dismal reality he sees.

On both sides of the building, dark, narrow alleys run into "murky canyons of tangled clotheslines, garbage cans and sinister lattice-work of neighboring fire escapes." The meaning of these alleys is clear if the reader recalls Tom's picture of "Death Valley," where cats were trapped and killed by a vicious dog. The predicament becomes a symbol of his factory work, murderous to his creative imagination. For Laura, the alley represents the ugly world from which she retreats to gaze into her tiny glass figures. For Amanda, too, the alley is the world of her present hopeless poverty and confusion from which she retreats into her make-believe world of memory and pretence. Inside the apartment, where she tries to create an illusion of gentility, her husband's portrait grins at her futile efforts.

The apartment is entered by a fire escape, "a structure whose name is a touch of accidental poetic truth, for all those huge buildings are always burning with the slow and implacable fires of human desperation." On this fire escape, Tom Wingfield seeks liberation from his private hell. It is no mere coincidence that this play's solution (like those of *Battle of Angels* and *Stairs to the Roof*) centers around the stairway. Stairs are the tangible sign of man's change in levels of reality.

It would seem that every item of the setting is symbolic—even the Paradise Dance Hall, across the alley. There sexual gratification provides the cliff-dwellers of the neighborhood a temporary paradise. In their moments of closeness, they achieve the escape that Tom finds in his movies and poetry.

The story, characterization, and setting of this play combine to form a "static" drama, a technique Williams has used in other plays, including the rewrite of *Battle of Angels*. Action is softened by this "patina" of time and distance; framed in memory, it becomes more artistic. The interest of this play depends on neither incident nor situation. Unlike most of Williams' other works that are charged with sensationalism and sex, this story holds the audience by the revelation of quiet and ordinary truths. This play, unique among Williams' dramas, combines poetic and unrealistic techniques with grim naturalism to achieve a gossamer effect of compassion, fragility, and frustration, typical of Tennessee Williams at his most sensitive and natural best. The play is his most effective poetic work.

Cinematic Elements in *The Glass Menagerie*

George Brandt

Moviemakers regularly adapt plays to the screen, but according to George Brandt, not much film technique has moved to the stage. Brandt suggests that Tennessee Williams counters this trend by employing many filmic elements in his plays, particularly *The Glass Menagerie*. Brandt identifies Williams's use of flashbacks, close-ups, and cinematic breaks of time. Additionally, the playwright's use of lighting parallels the film style of low-key lighting, soft focus, fade-ins, and fade-outs.

Brandt argues that Williams's original idea of projecting statements and images on a large background screen was not only inspired by the titles in silent films, it was also to be used like them to pull together episodes and clarify thought processes or comment on the action. Another film element in *The Glass Menagerie* is the mime sequence, when Tom makes his final break from the family. Brandt likens this scene to a cinematic nonsynchronous sequence of people without naturalistic sounds, accompanied by voice-over. For Brandt, much of the play's freshness stems from Williams's use of filmic devices.

George Brandt is a professor of radio, film, and television at the University of Bristol in England. He has served as the director of films for the British Broadcasting Corporation. He is the author of *British Television Drama* and a contributor to *The Cambridge Guide to World Theatre* and *The International Dictionary of the Theatre.*

Ever since the introduction of sound made the all-talking movie a commercial *sine qua non,* the American film industry has been indebted to the theatre for a good deal of its raw material. The ready-made plot and dialogue of successful

From "Cinematic Structure in the Work of Tennessee Williams," by George Brandt, in *American Theatre,* edited by John Russell Brown and Bernard Harris, Stratford-upon-Avon Studies, no. 10. Copyright ©1967 by Edward Arnold (Publishers) Ltd. Reprinted by permission of the publisher.

stage plays—and their equally ready-made publicity—were too good a bet for Hollywood to miss in its years of glory; and even in the latter years of decline the practice of making 'the film of the play' has continued. A long line of stage drama (often adapted merely in the rudimentary sense of being broken down into camera set-ups, with some establishing shots thrown in and some exterior sequences added to 'open up the action') stretches across the American screen all the way from *The Last of Mrs. Cheyney* and *Quality Street* to *The Moon is Blue*, from *Arsenic and Old Lace* and *Born Yesterday* to *Bus Stop*. Even the film musical (not primarily a literary form) as often as not began life on the stage: *Oklahoma!, West Side Story* and *South Pacific* are cases in point. Film theorists may frown on the practice, and it is true that it has contributed to keeping the American film dialogue-bound. But then, original film scripts have frequently been as guilty in this respect.

What in turn has the cinema given back to the American theatre? Not much. In view of the vast output of the American film industry (497 feature films were made in 1952, before the great decline set in) its impact upon the stage has been remarkably small. The general conception of plot structure, characterization and dialogue-writing has been coloured only to a minimal extent by the new techniques of dramatic story-telling opened up, at least potentially, by the younger medium.

What are these new techniques? Ever since [American motion picture director D.W.] Griffith, the cinema has been known to enjoy the greatest freedom in time and space, largely as a result of the editing process, even though film-makers might often neglect these new opportunities. The film can make unexpected connections, reverse the flow of time, break down complex events into significant details, leap from China to Peru, or look at causality from a fresh angle. The formal changes brought about by the use of real locations, the big close-up, the inclusion of slices of life have made new dramatic structures possible. . . .

It is Thomas Lanier Williams, better known as Tennessee Williams, who of all American playwrights has most effectively learnt the lessons in freedom that the cinema has to teach. He has been orientated towards the cinema for a very long time. A biographer of his tells us that the young Williams was a great movie addict while still at high school. 'During the years in St. Louis, out of loneliness and the desire to es-

cape from home, he spent much of his leisure time in cine-
mas. The quality of the presentation did not often matter'. The
imaginative hold that films had on him then is reflected
dearly enough in Tom, the narrator in the transparently autobiographical *Glass Menagerie*. Frequently nagged at by his
mother for spending so much of his time in the cinema, Tom
replies, 'Adventure is something I don't have much of at work,
so I go to the movies . . . I like a lot of adventure'. Here the author is plainly speaking for himself as an adolescent.

Williams broke through as a writer not for the theatre but
for the cinema to begin with: he was a contract script writer
for M-G-M in 1943. It was not a particularly happy period of
his career; his writing assignments turned out to be flops. His
original screen play *The Gentleman Caller* was rejected by
his somewhat short-sighted employers. However, the script
proved to be capable of being adapted to the stage, the reverse
of the customary procedure; and there, under the new name
of *The Glass Menagerie*, it put its author in the front rank of
American dramatists during its New York run in 1945. . . .

THE CINEMATIC STRUCTURE OF *THE GLASS MENAGERIE*

Quite the most cinematic of Williams's plays is *The Glass Menagerie*—which is not surprising seeing it was first conceived in screen terms. A 'memory play', it employs the double vision, both realistic and romantic, that [Arthur] Miller
was to cast over *A Memory of Two Mondays*. It has a narrator who introduces and comments upon the action, as does
Alfieri in *A View from the Bridge*. Miller may have been influenced in the latter play by Williams and other exponents
of the first-person-singular style of dramatic narration; at
any rate, both Miller and Williams have adapted that oldest
of cinematic tricks, the flashback, to the stage. *The Glass Menagerie* is infinitely more subjective than either of Miller's
plays: it contains sizable slabs of autobiography. Just as
Thomas Lanier Williams had worked during the Depression
as a clerk for the International Shoe Company in St. Louis,
Tom, the narrator, works for the 'Continental Shoemakers' in
the same city; he lives an intense imaginative life (we have
already mentioned his movie-going habits) and he attempts
to write in order to achieve some sort of inner freedom from
a stifling environment, exactly as Williams had done at that
period in his career. And just as Tom's sister Laura cannot
cope with life and is frightened of all human contacts, re-

treating into the fantasy world of her glass toys which symbolize her fragility (and to a lesser extent, that of Tom and Amanda as well), Williams's sister Rose was suffering from schizophrenia in real life; in 1937 she was committed to a mental hospital. Finally, Amanda Wingfield—surely one of Williams's most three-dimensional creations—contains recognizable features of his own mother.

The memory action is seen from Tom's point of view—opening and finishing as it were in close-up on the narrator. The feeling that runs through the play justifies the flashback device. This cinematic breaking up of the flow of time casts a veil of nostalgia over the events of the past; and as Williams points out in his Production Notes to *The Glass Menagerie,* nostalgia is the play's first condition. The feeling matters more than the mere outer action.

The typical interior-exterior setting serves the double purpose of peeling away the defences that Laura has built up against the world and of penetrating into the mind of the narrator, Tom. The vision of the play is dim with tears, with feelings of loss, sorrow, guilt and resentment. The fire-escape, a perfectly literal piece of domestic architecture, also stands for escape from family ties.

> The scene is memory and is therefore non-realistic. Memory takes a lot of poetic licence. It omits some details; others are exaggerated, according to the emotional value of the articles it touches, for memory is seated predominantly in the heart. The interior is therefore rather dim and poetic. (From the stage directions for scene i)

WILLIAMS'S CINEMATIC USE OF LIGHTING

More than most plays, *The Glass Menagerie* would suffer from being presented without any technical aids. Its delicacy, its dependence for theatrical effectiveness on tone rather than plot do not make it a suitable vehicle for, let us say, sceneryless production. In building up the atmosphere for the play, Williams falls back to quite an exceptional degree on sensitive lighting. He has spelt out his requirements in the Production Notes:

> Shafts of light are focused on selected areas or actors, sometimes in contradistinction to what is the apparent centre. For instance, in the quarrel scene between TOM and AMANDA, in which LAURA has no active part, the clearest pool of light is on her figure. This is also true of the supper scene, when her silent figure on the sofa should remain the visual centre. The

light upon LAURA should be distinct from the others, having a peculiar pristine clarity such as light used in early religious portraits of female saints or madonnas. A certain correspondence to light in religious paintings, such as El Greco's, where the figures are radiant in atmosphere that is relatively dusky, could be effectively used throughout the play.

If this atmosphere is produced by what in camera terms would be low-key lighting and soft-focus photography, including the frequent use of a diffusion disc, Williams also gives us the stage equivalent to certain standard opticals. The memory action fades in, like the beginning of the normal film sequence, by the light coming on gradually behind the gauze fourth wall that at first separates the Wingfield interior from the auditorium; at the end of Tom's introductory speech, the wall is flown slowly. The reverse occurs as the play finishes: Laura blows out the candles and the gauze wall is dropped back into the scene again—fade-out. Not only the beginning and the conclusion of the play but all of its seven scenes (with the exception of scene v which brings down the interval curtain) follow the same pattern. Williams actually uses the film term 'fade out', and he says of the dying away of the light in the final scene, in a sense slightly different from its technical meaning in films: 'THE SCENE DISSOLVES'. The fading in and out of light as such is, of course, not peculiar to Williams's stagecraft; but he uses it in an almost cinematic way to represent thought processes, the rhythm of Tom's memory.

WILLIAMS'S SCREEN DEVICE

Few critics have paid any attention to Williams's intended use of projections in the play, largely I suppose because they are always omitted in production. His idea here is obviously rather different from [Bertolt] Brecht's alienating use of a similar device: Williams is far from opposing emotional audience involvement as such. Brecht claimed these very un-Williamsian virtues for the projection of titles (at a fairly early stage in the development of his theories, in 1931):

> The orthodox playwright's objection to the titles is that the dramatist ought to say everything that has to be said in the action, that the text must express everything within its own confines. . . . But this way of subordinating everything to a single idea . . . is something that the new school of play-writing must reject. . . .
>
> Some exercise in complex seeing is needed. . . . As he reads

the projections on the screen the spectator adopts an attitude of smoking-and-watching.

Certainly it is no part of Williams's intentions to create an audience of cigar-smoking children of the scientific age. But are there not at least some hints of a Brechtian function—a 'literarization' of the drama—in what he had hoped the titles would do for the play?

> In an episodic play, such as this, the basic structure or narrative line may be obscured from the audience; the effect may seem fragmentary rather than architectural. This may not be the fault of the play so much as a lack of attention in the audience. The legend or image upon the screen will strengthen the effect of what is merely illusion in the writing and allow the primary point to be made more simply and lightly than if the entire responsibility were on the spoken lines. Aside from this structural value, I think the screen will have a definite emotional appeal, less definable but just as important.
>
> (Production Notes to *The Glass Menagerie.*)

The atmospheric use of titles may be un-Brechtian but the title as a pointer to the meaning of a scene is not. Williams's motivation even in this latter respect was of course different from Brecht's—a fear that the text on its own might not quite make the intended impact. One can see the reason for this fear. *The Glass Menagerie,* structurally, is in essence a short story, or if you like a one-act play, expanded to full-length proportions. Its core, the actual storyline, is contained in Laura's confrontation with the Gentleman Caller, i.e. in scenes vi and vii. All the previous scenes are narrative, not dramatic. This loose welding together of scenes derives a good deal from filmic structure which—as in much of Antonioni's and Fellini's work, for instance—can sustain interest by the recording of atmosphere or the observation of the minute details of behaviour.

The analogy with Brecht's titles may not take us very far in evaluating Williams's screen device. It does, however, suggest a certain irony in the author's viewpoint which is only too easily ignored in production. Another comparison may make this even clearer. The screens—which, it is to be noted, are to carry images as well as legends—bear a striking resemblance to, and were quite probably inspired by, silent film titles. As a matter of fact, some of them read exactly like such titles: 'AFTER THE FIASCO—'. . . 'YOU THINK I'M IN LOVE WITH CONTINENTAL SHOEMAKERS?'. . . 'I DON'T SUPPOSE YOU REMEMBER ME AT ALL!'. . . 'A PRETTY TRAP'. . . or (a very authentic note this)—'TERROR!' Some titles are obviously, deliberately, pre-posterous. In scene vi a title reads, 'AH!', in scene vii there is a title, 'HA!' Like silent film titles, these legends supply thought processes or they comment on the action. Some-times a transparently ironical point is made (and here we are quite close to the epic-theatre title), e.g. 'SUSPENSION OF A PUBLIC SERVICE', flashed on the screen just as the electric light goes off in the Wingfield flat. Images too are frequently given an ironical colouring, as when a young man with a bunch of flowers or a glamour-magazine cover are projected to sym-bolize Amanda Wingfield's pathetically unreal expectations and aspirations, or when Jim O'Connor's brasher but proba-bly just as unrealistic ambitions are represented by a picture of an executive at a desk. Sometimes the images supply a naïve touch of poetry: blue roses are shown on the screen to underline the fact that 'Blue Roses' had been Jim's nickname for Laura at high school, a misunderstanding of 'pleurosis'.

On the whole we need not regret the practice of omitting the projections when *The Glass Menagerie* is produced. But they do point to a greater detachment on the author's part than is sometimes supposed, a detachment that keeps his nostalgia from becoming too cloying.

WILLIAMS'S USE OF MIME

Another touch of silent film technique is very movingly intro-duced at the end of the play. Tom has at last decided to make the final break with his family. While the screen legend reads, 'AND SO GOOD-BYE . . .' a silent mime takes place on stage.

> The interior scene is played as though viewed through sound-proof glass. AMANDA appears to be making a comforting speech to LAURA who is huddled upon the sofa. Now that we cannot hear the mother's speech, her silliness is gone and she has dignity and tragic beauty. LAURA's dark hair hides her face until at the end of the speech she lifts it to smile at her mother. AMANDA's gestures are slow and graceful, almost dancelike, as she comforts the daughter.

This passage works like a piece of silent film, or more ac-curately, like a non-synchronous sequence in a sound film where instead of a naturalistic track we hear the narrator's voice. As in a film we are moved not by the persons them-selves but by the images of persons—images here filtered through Tom's vision. As the two women attain the perspec-tive of memory in his, and thereby in the audience's, mind we are reconciled to the structural deficiency in the play of which the author was himself so clearly aware.

Has the injection of filmic elements into Tennessee Williams's dramatic writings been beneficial or harmful? Any borrowings from related arts that can add to the vocabulary of the drama must surely be welcomed—as long as they do not run counter to the basic laws of the stage. The technical facilities of the modern theatre enable the playwright to do certain things not possible before, or at any rate not possible to the same level of perfection; and Tennessee Williams's acute visual and aural sensibility enables him to take full advantage of these facilities, with a consequent enrichment not merely of the form of his drama but of its content as well. But there is a danger in using the incidentals of drama—atmospherics, picture-making, the building up of sound effects—to disguise profound structural weaknesses. Even *The Glass Menagerie* and *A Streetcar Named Desire,* still to this day Williams's best plays and certainly his most successful ones, are not altogether immune to criticism on this score.

The Evolution of
The Glass Menagerie

Lester A. Beaurline

Lester Beaurline compares the four different versions
of *The Glass Menagerie* that Williams produced: a
short story called "Portrait of a Girl in Glass," inspired
by the playwright's sister; a 60-page one-act play in
five scenes; a 105-page "reading version" play that
was written over eight to ten years; and an acting
version of the play that was produced in New York
and on the road. Beaurline's comparison of the
different versions reflects the changes Williams
made to strengthen action and meaning.

Beaurline also delineates the progression of Jim's
character from a masculine, potential lover in the
short story to a naive positive thinker in the acting
version. In addition to changes in dialogue and character, Beaurline discusses the removal of the reading
version's screen device, originally intended to project
images and printed legends.

Lester Beaurline is a professor of English at the
University of Virginia. In addition to numerous critical editions of plays, Beaurline has published *Jonson
and Elizabethan Comedy.*

"Not even daring to stretch her small hands out!—nobody,
not even the rain, has such small hands." Tennessee
Williams scrawled these words from e.e. cummings at the top
of the last page of *The Glass Menagerie* sometime after finishing the one-act play that was to grow into his first successful work. The quotation suggests the gentle, elegiac tone
that he tried to attain, and since the last half of the passage
survived as the play's epigraph, it apparently expressed
Williams' later feelings too. The fragile pathos of Laura
Wingfield's life was Williams' original inspiration in his short

From "*The Glass Menagerie:* From Story to Play," by Lester A. Beaurline, *Modern
Drama,* vol. 8, no. 2 (Fall 1965), pp. 142–49. Reprinted by permission of *Modern Drama.*

story, "Portrait of a Girl in Glass," and theater audiences continue to respond to the basic human appeal of the play.

In "Portrait" the narrator feels compassion for Laura, who "made no positive motion toward the world but stood at the edge of the water, so to speak, with feet that anticipated too much cold to move." In this early story we can already recognize Williams' other trademarks: the theme of Tom's flight from "a dead but beautiful past into a live but ugly and meaningless present" (William Sharp, *TDR*, VI, March, 1962, 161), the images of leaves torn from their branches, the hundreds of little transparent pieces of glass, the tired old music of the dead past, and the emotional undercurrent of sexual passion roaring through the entire story. These themes, I suppose, show Williams' kinship with D.H. Lawrence; and Tom, no doubt, suggests the figure of Paul Morrell or Aaron Sisson. But the later revisions show Williams' real talents as a playwright, none of which he inherits from Lawrence: his breadth of sympathy, his sense of humor, his brilliant dialogue, and his talent for building highly charged dramatic scenes.

FOUR STAGES OF THE PLAY'S COMPOSITION

Evidence survives for at least four stages in the composition of *The Glass Menagerie:* (1) The sixteen page story entitled "Portrait of a Girl in Glass" (written before 1943 and published in *One Arm and Other Stories,* 1948), where attention is on Laura, the narrator's sister.

(2) A sixty-page one-act play in five scenes, of which twenty-one pages survive in the C. Waller Barrett Library at the University of Virginia. It is clear from the existing fragments that Williams had the main lines of his play firmly in hand at this stage. Here the clash between Tom and Amanda, the painful relationship between Amanda and Laura, and the contrast between Jim and Tom have become as important as Laura herself. This script was probably written before Williams went to California to work on a movie script in 1943 and before he worked up a synopsis for a film named *The Gentleman Caller.*

(3) A 105-page play manuscript, now in the C. Waller Barrett Library at the University of Virginia. This complex document contains ten kinds of paper, is written on at least six different typewriters, and has four different kinds of handwritten pencil or ink revisions. It may represent about eight

to ten layers of revision, but for the sake of clarity, I will refer to only the final stage of the third version: the manuscript as it stood when Williams sent it off to his agent in the fall of 1943. He called this the "reading version," and it is very close to the Random House edition, published in 1945 and reprinted by New Directions in 1949. However, this printed edition (which unfortunately has gotten into the college anthologies) contains several errors and a few alterations. The long version of the manuscript is in seven scenes and is a development and expansion of episodes in the one-act version. At this stage the major emphasis in the play is on memory, Tom's memory. It is a play about growing up as Tom must recognize the fatal choice between Laura's glass animals and Jim's gross materialism.

(4) The acting version, published by the Dramatists Play Service in 1948 (and revised again sometime in the mid-fifties). This purports to be "a faithful indication of the way the play was produced in New York and on the road" by the original company. Many changes have been made in the stage directions and details of the dialogue. One new scene was added, and over 1100 verbal changes appear in the dialogue alone. I think that Williams is now finished with the play and that the fourth version represents his final intentions. Therefore a responsible editor of an anthology should *not* reprint the old "reading version," and a critic ignores the acting version at his peril.

CHANGES IN DIALOGUE

Changes in Tom's last speech epitomize all the revision in the play, so it is worth examining a long passage that closes the "Girl in Glass."

> Not very long after that I lost my job at the warehouse. I was fired for writing a poem on the lid of a shoe-box. I left Saint Louis and took to moving around. The cities swept about me like dead leaves, leaves that were brightly colored but torn away from the branches. My nature changed. I grew to be firm and sufficient.

> In five years' time I had nearly forgotten home. I had to forget it, I couldn't carry it with me. But once in a while, usually in a strange town before I have found companions, the shell of deliberate hardness is broken through. A door comes softly and irresistibly open. I hear the tired old music my unknown father left in the place he abandoned as faithlessly as I. I see the faint and sorrowful radiance of the glass, hundreds of lit-

tle transparent pieces of it in very delicate colors. I hold my breath, for if my sister's face appears among them—the night is hers!

In the second draft (the one-act version), Williams heightened Tom's emotional tension between his necessary cruelty and his affection for the ones he is hurting. His cruel side comes out when he says, "Then I escaped. Without a word of goodbye, I descended the steps of the fire-escape for the last time." The incestuous implications of the speech become more explicit: "In five years time I have nearly forgotten home. But there are nights when memory is stronger. I cannot hold my shoulder to the door, the door comes softly but irresistibly open. . . . I hold my breath. I reach for a cigarette. I buy a drink, I speak to the nearest stranger. For if that vision goes on growing clearer, the mist will divide upon my sister's face, watching gently and daring to ask for nothing. Then it's too much: my manhood is undone and the night is hers."

In the third version, the speech is more integrated with the scene. Amanda had just shouted at him, "Go then! Then go to the moon! —you selfish dreamer." So Tom begins his epilogue with "I didn't go to the moon. I went much further—for time is the longest distance between two places." (We should recall that Amanda had asked Laura to wish on the moon before the gentleman caller came.) Another unifying detail was added at the end. Laura, in pantomime, blows out the candles, which like the moon have come to suggest her hopes, the romantic half-light, similar to the glow that came across the alley from the Paradise Ballroom. She had already blown out her candles in the second version, but in the third, Tom says, "anything that can blow your candles out! (LAURA BENDS OVER THE CANDLES) Blow out your candles, Laura!—for nowadays the world is lit by lightning! Blow out your candles, Laura,—and so goodbye. . . . (SHE BLOWS THE CANDLES OUT. THE SCENE DISSOLVES.)" So the dialogue and action reinforce each other. . . .

SCRIPT CHANGES REFLECT WILLIAMS' GROWTH AS A DRAMATIST

There are a hundred ways that the body of the play depicts Tom's awareness of the essential hopelessness of the Wingfield family and the essential deadness of their beautiful memories. I will not explain how each detail came into the script; two more examples will have to suffice. One of the greatest moments in modern theater occurs when Amanda comes on stage to greet Laura's gentleman caller. Nobody says a word for a few seconds; everyone's eyes are fixed on Amanda's dress—the old ball dress that she wore when she led the cotillion years ago. Before age had yellowed this dress she had twice won the cakewalk, and she had worn it to the Governor's ball in Jackson. The dress, at this moment, suggests the utter futility of Amanda's efforts to find a husband for her daughter. She defeats her own purposes; she cannot resist pretending that the gentleman caller has come to call on her, just as seventeen of them came one afternoon on Blue Mountain. Tom is shocked and embarrassed. The grotesque sight leaves Jim speechless, and he is a young man proud of his high-school training in public speaking. Meanwhile Laura lies in her bedroom, sick with fear.

 THE ORIGINS OF *THE GLASS MENAGERIE*

In an interview in the Paris Review *reprinted in Albert J. Devlin's* Conversations with Tennessee Williams, *Williams mentions how the idea for* The Glass Menagerie *evolved slowly from his short story "Portrait of a Girl in Glass."*

The idea for *The Glass Menagerie* came very slowly, much more slowly than *Streetcar* for example. I think I worked on *Menagerie* longer than any other play. I didn't think it'd ever be produced. I wasn't writing it for that purpose. I wrote it first as a short story called "Portrait of a Girl in Glass," which is, I believe, one of my best stories. I guess *Menagerie* grew out of the intense emotions I felt seeing my sister's mind begin to go.

Mr. Williams did not achieve such a theatrical triumph by writing with his guts or by pouring out his uncontrolled libido. In the short story, he tried to make Laura pathetic by dressing her in one of her mother's old gowns, and Tom is momentarily surprised by her appearance when she opens the door. In the one-act version, Amanda's memories of Blue Mountain are written into the script, and Laura is furnished with a new dress, but now she is lame. By the third version (possibly in the second, too, but I cannot be sure because the relevant pages of the second version do not survive), Amanda wears the old dress and becomes a coquette. In the fourth version, Williams softens the effect slightly and adds a little more to the irony by a brief exchange between Tom and his mother. At the peak of Tom's embarrassment, after the pregnant pause, he says:

> Mother, you look so pretty.
> AMANDA. You know, that's the first compliment you ever paid me. I wish you'd look pleasant when you're about to say something pleasant, so I could expect it.

Then Amanda swings into her girlish chatter. These last additions seem to assure the audience that Tom is genuinely shocked but that he is trying to cover up his feelings. At the same time the audience has to have evidence that Amanda is not completely out of her mind. She can still recognize a hollow compliment, and she can return the jibe.

By typical use of his dramatic talents, Williams makes the audience conscious of several characters' feelings at the same time, like a juggler keeping four balls in the air. Each revision puts another ball in the air or increases the specific pressure. We are never allowed to forget the tension between Tom and his mother, and the scene strongly suggests that Laura's anxiety and withdrawal may have been caused by her aggressive mother. The final image of Amanda in the Epilogue is that of a comforter and protector of Laura. She is dignified and tragic. But she is most vividly depicted in the middle of the play as a vigorous, silly, and pathetic old woman. Fearing that her daughter might become an old maid, she arranges the visit of a gentleman caller. Yet, she cannot resist the temptation to smother her daughter and relive her Blue Mountain days; she vicariously seduces the man herself. She has to keep bringing the dead but beautiful past into the present; Tom must go into the ugly but live future. He must break out of the coffin and leave his sister behind in darkness.

CHANGES IN JIM'S CHARACTER

The transmutations of Jim O'Connor illustrate Mr. Williams' talent for depicting minor characters. At the start, Jim had a warm masculine nature; he was a potential lover and a Lawrencian hero. "Jim was a big red-haired Irishman who had the scrubbed and polished look of well-kept chinaware. His big square hands seemed to have a direct and very innocent hunger for touching friends. He was always clapping them on your arms or shoulders and they burned through the cloth of your shirt like plates taken out of an oven."

In the one-act version, Jim becomes slightly hollow when

he tries to persuade Tom to study public speaking. Then, in the reading version, Jim assimilates some of the play's nostalgic tone when he becomes an ex-high-school hero. The distracting homosexual suggestions disappear, and now Tom was "valuable to him as someone who could remember his former glory, who had seen him win basketball games and the silver cup in debating." On the edge of failure, Jim seems to put on his hearty good nature. He is more often named the "gentleman caller" than Jim O'Connor, a detail that helps to transform him into an idea in the head of Amanda, just as Laura becomes an image of "Blue-roses" in his mind. Also in the reading version Jim first talks enthusiastically about the world of the present and future—the world that Amanda and Laura cannot enter. When he should be romancing with Laura, he orates on the Wrigley Building, the Century of Progress, and the future of television. "I wish to be ready to go up right along with it. Therefore I'm planning to get in on the ground floor. In fact I've already made the right connections and all that remains is for the industry itself to get under way! Full steam—*(His eyes are starry.)* *Knowledge—*Zzzzzp! *Money—*Zzzzzp!—*Power!* That's the cycle democracy is built on!" He clumsily breaks Laura's unicorn, and he awkwardly kisses her.

Jim finally impresses us as a dehumanized figure, an unromantic voice of power and cliché; his sex appeal has been carefully removed, and his insensitive words, and power of positive thinking take its place. Consequently, with every change he suits Laura less and less, and he embodies Tom's "celotex interior" more and more. In the finished play, Amanda's mental projection of the old-fashioned gentleman caller reveals him to be Tom's brute reality.

CHANGES IN STAGE DIRECTIONS

Other important changes are found in the stage directions, especially the visual images and printed legends that Williams experimented with and rejected—wisely, I think. One legend, "A Souvenir," survives in the fragments of the one-act play (at the beginning of what was eventually scene viii), and the earliest forms of the reading version show an attempted use of a blackboard on which Tom wrote in chalk such things as *"Blue Roses"* (scene ii), *"Campaign"* (scene iii), and *"Où sont les Neiges d'antan"* (scene i). The completed reading version projected these legends by means of the much discussed "screen device," possibly conceived in the film synopsis that preceded the reading version. Williams said, "The legend or image upon the screen will strengthen the effect of what is merely allusion [*sic*] in the writing and allow the primary point to be made more simply and lightly than if the entire responsibility were on the spoken lines." The real weakness of the device lies in the author's anxiousness and small confidence in his audience. "In an episodic play, such as this, the basic structure or narrative line may be observed from the audience; the effect may seem fragmentary rather than architectural. This may not be the fault of the play so much as a lack of attention in the audience." And I suspect that if the screen device has ever been tried, it distracted the audience from the actors, just as the lighting can distract unless it is used sparingly. Father's lighted picture seems to work once or twice, but I doubt if similar mechanical marvels add to the unified effect. At any rate, Williams says he does not regret the omission of the screen device in the first New York production, because he saw that Laurette Taylor's powerful performance "made it suitable to have the utmost simplicity in physical production." [Set designer] Jo Melziner's two scrims no doubt also helped persuade him. An air of unreality is one thing but pretentious pointing out of meaning is another.

Williams' most successful revisions of stage directions unobtrusively change the story's matter-of-fact tone into memory. The narrator of the story becomes the presenter of the play, and significant stage properties appear in the big scene: the blasted candelabra from the altar of the Church of the Heavenly Rest, the ice cream, fruit punch, and macaroons. In the reading version the ice cream was replaced with dandelion wine (for a mock communion?), and Amanda "baptizes" herself with lemonade—all of which contributes to the vague religious impression of the scene. No one explicitly defines the meaning of these symbols, but they quietly suggest that the events represent Laura's pitiful initiation rites; this is as close as she will ever come to the altar of love, because Jim is no Savior. She must blow her candles out. The empty ceremony is over.

D.H. Lawrence's Work Influenced Tennessee Williams

Norman J. Fedder

In *The Glass Menagerie* Williams makes several references to the English novelist D.H. Lawrence. Norman J. Fedder elaborates on Lawrence's influence on the American playwright. Although the bleak tenement setting of the play recalls Lawrence's industrial setting in *Lady Chatterley's Lover*, it is with Lawrence's *Sons and Lovers* that *The Glass Menagerie* can be most closely compared. Fedder writes that both works involve similar character types: Amanda Wingfield and Gertrude Morel marry beneath them, generating disastrous, broken families; Tom Wingfield and Paul Morel both have poetic natures limited by family responsibilities; and Laura Wingfield and Miriam Leivers both struggle with normal social relationships.

Fedder suggests that the authors shared early bad experiences with their fathers and play this fact out in their works. Moreover, both authors write about doomed and abortive love relationships.

Norman Fedder is a professor of drama at Kansas State University, Manhattan. As a playwright, his most recent works include *Custody, Abraham! Abraham!*, and *A Light to the Nations*.

It was [*The Glass Menagerie*] which, as Lawrence's *Sons and Lovers* did for its author, won Williams critical and public acclaim for the first time. This was not the playwright's initial attempt to work with closely autobiographical materials. The plot and many of its details had been anticipated by situations and references throughout his previous work: The figures of the crippled, delicate young girl (Laura); of the

From *The Influence of D.H. Lawrence on Tennessee Williams* by Norman J. Fedder (The Hague, the Netherlands: Mouton, 1966). Copyright ©1966 by Mouton & Co. Reprinted by permission of Mouton de Gruyter, a division of Walter de Gruyter & Co.

virile young man (Jim), whom she desires but cannot cope with; of the sensitive artist-brother (Tom), who looks on, sympathetic but helpless; of the illusion-ridden aristocratic mother (Amanda); and of the father who has deserted his family (the elder Wingfield)—all have their prototypes in the stories "Portrait of a Girl in Glass" and "The Resemblance between a Violin Case and a Coffin", in the poems "Cortege" and "Orpheus Descending", and in the one act play "The Long Goodbye".

Williams' description of the tenement setting of the play embodies a hatred of industrial civilization which recalls Lawrence's dismal portrait, in *Lady Chatterley's Lover*, of the factory-ridden Tevershall countryside:

> *The Wingfield apartment is in the rear of the building, one of those vast hive-like conglomerations of cellular living-units that flower as warty growths in overcrowded urban centers of lower middle-class population and are symptomatic of the impulse of the largest and fundamentally enslaved section of American society to avoid fluidity and differentiation and to exist and function as one interfused mass of automatism. The apartment faces an alley and is entered by a fire-escape, a structure whose name is a touch of accidental poetic truth, for all of these huge buildings are always burning with the slow and implacable fires of human desperation.*

> The car ploughed uphill through the long squalid straggle of Tevershall, the blackened brick dwellings, the black slate roofs glistening their sharp edges, the mud black with coal-dust, the pavements wet and black. It was as if dismalness had soaked through everything. The utter negation of natural beauty, the utter negation of the gladness of life, the utter absence of the instinct for shapely beauty which every bird and beast has, the utter death of the human intuitive faculty was appalling.

SIMILARITIES IN CHARACTER DEVELOPMENT

However, *The Glass Menagerie* compares most closely with Lawrence's *Sons and Lovers*. Both works focus on situations involving a domineering mother, a weak father, an artistically inclined son, and the abortive relationship between a virginal girl and the virile young man she loves.

Amanda Wingfield corresponds with Gertrude Morel as—in the words of Lawrence—"a woman of character and refinement who goes into the lower class, and [who] has no satisfaction in her own life". Both women—after being courted by a number of men socially and intellectually their equals—had suddenly fallen in love with a social inferior whom they met at a dance. His violently sensual nature stood out in sharp contrast to their own inhibited sensibilities. An instantaneous attraction of opposites precipitated marriages of incompatibles, doomed to the continuous misery of mutual incomprehension.

Tom Wingfield compares with Paul Morel. Both are deeply enmeshed in neurotic relationships involving their mothers and a delicate young girl; both have artistic ambitions which are retarded by the necessity of their contributing to the family weal through the enervating tedium of factory work. An alternative counterpart to Paul Morel in the play is Jim, the gentleman caller, who resembles the former as the delicate young girl's suitor.

Finally, the fragile delicacy of Laura Wingfield and Miriam Leivers corresponds rather closely:

> A fragile, unearthly prettiness.... Laura... is like a piece of translucent glass touched by light, given a momentary radiance, not actual, not lasting.

> Her [Miriam's] beauty—that of a shy, wild, quiveringly sensitive thing....

> Miriam was exceedingly sensitive.... The slightest grossness made her recoil almost in anguish.

Both find it difficult to adjust to normal social relationships—each more at home in a less threatening, non-human world: Laura's beloved collection of little glass animals, Miriam's fixation with the flowers surrounding her woodland home. Both sense the inadequacy of their fragmented natures and would gladly be aroused to sensual awareness were they only emotionally capable of it. However, the claims of the flesh are too much for them. The virile young men—Jim and Paul—who attempt to awaken them, only meet with failure. There is, it is true, a momentary communion of the spirit—when their lovers share with them the joys of the girls' private worlds.

But Miriam's incapacity to give herself freely in a sexual union makes her relationship with Paul impossible: "the dark . . . fire of desire did not belong to her."

And Laura's dream of a possible relationship with Jim is shattered by the unexpected revelation of his forthcoming marriage to another woman. Yet we know that her excessive spirituality must frustrate any normal love union. Amanda speaks for both Laura and Miriam, I think, when she emphatically counters Tom's apostrophe to instinctual values—

a Lawrence-derived dialogue which we have above desig-
nated "the flesh-spirit dialectic."

TOM: Man is by instinct a lover, a hunter, a fighter, and none
of these instincts are given much play at the warehouse!

AMANDA: Man is by instinct! Don't quote instinct to me! Instinct is something that people have got away from! It belongs
to animals! Christian adults don't want it!

TOM: What do Christian adults want, then, Mother?

AMANDA: Superior things! Things of the mind and the spirit!
Only animals have to satisfy instincts! Surely your aims are
somewhat higher than theirs! Than monkeys—pigs—

TOM: I reckon they're not.

THE AUTHORS' SIMILAR ATTITUDES TOWARD THEIR FATHERS

The plot similarities between *Sons and Lovers* and *The Glass
Menagerie* derive no doubt from the striking parallels which
exist between the two authors' early environmental experiences. As we have indicated above, both writers had strongly
negative feelings toward their weak though tyrannical fathers. Rebelling against the vulgarity of the paternal figure,
they chose to identify themselves instead with the softer
qualities of femininity. Williams, therefore, has named his
mother and sister as two of the most significant influences
on his life; while Lawrence has acknowledged that his
mother and early love (Jessie Chambers) were crucial to his
emotional and intellectual development: Thus we can understand the central position of the mother and daughter-
girl friend and the relative unimportance of the fathers in
autobiographical play and novel.

It is interesting to note this early antagonism of Lawrence
and Williams toward the sensual male figure in the light of
their glorification of him in the bulk of their work. The para-
doxical fact is that Lawrence's and Williams' work represents a rebellion against their initial psychological predilec-
tions. As Harry T. Moore has observed apropos of Lawrence:

Arthur Lawrence is portrayed in his son's novel, *Sons and
Lovers*, as a brutalized drunkard. In later years Lawrence felt
that he had not understood his father because he had, in
childhood and youth, seen him through the prejudiced eyes
of his mother. . . .

Beyond the portrait of him in *Sons and Lovers*, which at the
realistic level perhaps helped Lawrence exorcise the father-

image, there seems to be a lingering influence of the father in the son's later worship of earth-men. . . .

The collier father . . . should be remembered as standing be-hind Lawrence ancestrally, as forever murmuring in his blood. The father in his bearded virility became, for the most part unconsciously perhaps, a kind of ideal to Lawrence, though except in conversation he would rarely have good words for his father as an individual: the deflected praise was symbolic, the worship of earth-bound peasant and simple Indian.

Similarly, Williams, in an early poem "Cortege", is severely critical of his father:

Cold, cold, cold
was the merciless blood of thy father.
By the halo of his breath
thy mother knew him,
by January she knew him,
and dreaded the knowledge . . .
She passed him and crept sidewise
down the stairs,
loathing the touch
of the doorknob he had clasped,
hating the napkin
he had used at the table
The children bolted their food
and played out-doors in winter
Hop-scotch took them
blocks away from their father.

But in *The Glass Menagerie,* a later work, the playwright pre-sents his father in a more favorable light. The elder Wing-field becomes the prototype for the irresponsible bohemian who figures so importantly in Williams' work. Tom's great ambition is to "follow . . . in my father's footsteps, attempting to find in motion what was lost in space"—which he does as the play concludes.

SIMILARITIES IN DRAMATIC SITUATION

The Williams play compares favorably with the Lawrence novel in its subtle rendering of an abortive relationship. But of course there is more to *Sons and Lovers* than the charac-ters, situations, and themes which we have thus far dis-cussed. A play must, of necessity, include less situational material. A dramatic work—taking into consideration the needs of stage presentation—requires a plot which must em-body a conflict situation sufficient to maintain an audience's interest not much longer than two hours. It must be, moreover, a situation which—in not much more than 100 pages, representing only those circumstances capable of being staged effectively—can fully realize the author's thematic intentions. Add to this the inability of the playwright, particularly in the realistic drama, to expatiate extensively on the thoughts and feelings of his characters; and it is understandable that many writers, eminently successful in the novel, have created plays of relatively small importance.

WILLIAMS'S DEBT TO LAWRENCE AND CHEKHOV

In Memoirs *Tennessee Williams acknowledges the influence of English novelist D.H. Lawrence, but he writes that Russian playwright Anton Chekhov is a greater influence.*

That summer I fell in love with the writing of Anton Chekhov, at least with his many short stories. They introduced me to a literary sensibility to which I felt a very close affinity at that time. Now I find that he holds too much in reserve. I still am in love with the delicate poetry of his writing and *The Sea Gull* is still, I think, the greatest of modern plays, with the possible exception of Brecht's *Mother Courage.*

It has often been said that Lawrence was my major literary influence. Well, Lawrence was, indeed, a highly *simpatico* figure in my literary upbringing, but Chekhov takes precedence as an influence—that is, if there has been any particular influence beside my own solitary bent—toward what I am not yet sure and probably never will be.

Such a writer was Lawrence, whose dramatic version of *Sons and Lovers, A Collier's Friday Night,* although effective in dialogue and individual scenes, leaves one with a sense of incompleteness, a feeling that only a part of the story has been told. The essence of Paul Morel's situation is not fully revealed in the incident in his life which Lawrence chooses to dramatize. The jealous conflict between mother and son ensuing from Ernest's (Paul's) neglect of his mother's baking bread because of his absorption with Maggie (Miriam) has its significance in its proper place within the greater fabric of the novel; but it is too trivial an incident to fully realize Paul's situation as son and lover, drawn out to its essential proportions in the novel.

Williams, on the other hand, in *The Glass Menagerie*—although having utilized an incident which might seem, from a superficial standpoint, equally trivial—has managed to capture the full substance of Laura's tragedy. This, since for Laura's hypersensitive nature, the momentary rejection by Jim is of the greatest significance. In *The Glass Menagerie* theme and form are effectively fused for the first time in a Williams work; and it continues to rank as one of his finest achievements.

Lawrence's influence on Williams is finally evidenced, as has been noted, in the reading habits with which the latter endows his alter ego:

> TOM: Yesterday you confiscated my books! You had the nerve to—
>
> AMANDA: I did. I took that horrible novel back to the library— That hideous book by that insane Mr. Lawrence.

CHRONOLOGY

1898

Spanish-American War; Tennessee Williams's father, Cornelius Williams, serves in the army.

1901

President William McKinley is assassinated.

1907

Edwina Dakin marries Cornelius Coffin Williams in Columbus, Mississippi.

1911

Thomas Lanier Williams is born in Columbus, Mississippi, the second of three children; older sister, Rose Isabel, born 1909; younger brother, Walter Dakin, born 1919.

1914

Panama Canal opens; World War I begins.

1919

Treaty of Versailles ends World War I; the Williams family moves to St. Louis.

1920

Women win the right to vote.

1927

The Jazz Singer is first talking movie.

1928

Williams travels to Europe with his Grandfather Dakin.

1929

Stock market crash begins the Great Depression; Williams graduates from University City High School and begins college at the University of Missouri.

1933

Williams's father withdraws him from college to work at the International Shoe Company.

1935

Works Progress Administration is formed; Social Security Act is passed; Williams suffers a nervous breakdown and is left with partial paralysis of his legs; during his recuperation, he collaborates with Bernice Dorothy Shapiro on *Cairo! Shanghai! Bombay!*

1936

Williams enters Washington University, St. Louis.

1937

Withdraws from Washington University and enrolls at the University of Iowa; Rose Williams undergoes a lobotomy to treat her emotional problems.

1938

Graduates from the University of Iowa with a degree in English.

1939

World War II begins with the German invasion of Poland; Williams meets Audrey Wood, his agent for thirty years, after winning a writing contest; first uses the name Tennessee on a published work, "The Field of Blue Children."

1940

Attends playwriting seminar at the New School for Social Research; *Battle of Angels* opens and quickly folds in Boston.

1941

Japanese attack Pearl Harbor; United States enters World War II.

1943

Works at MGM as a scriptwriter; writes a rejected script called *The Gentleman Caller.*

1944

Finishes *The Glass Menagerie*; the play opens at the Civic Theater in Chicago.

1945

WWII ends; *The Glass Menagerie* opens on Broadway, wins New York Drama Critics Circle Award.

1947

A Streetcar Named Desire begins a successful run on Broadway, wins Pulitzer Prize.

1949

NATO is founded.

1950–1953

McCarthyism and the Red Scare take hold in Washington; Korean War.

1951

The Rose Tattoo is a hit on Broadway and wins the Tony for the best play.

1952

Williams is elected to the National Institute of Arts and Letters.

1955

Cat on a Hot Tin Roof is staged successfully in New York City and wins Williams's second Pulitzer Prize; Williams's grandfather, the Reverend Walter Dakin, dies.

1957

Soviet Union launches *Sputnik*, the first man-made satellite; Cornelius Williams dies and Tennessee enters psychoanalysis; *Orpheus Descending* has a limited run in New York.

1959

Sweet Bird of Youth opens in New York; Williams sells the movie rights to the play for $400,000.

1960

The comedy *Period of Adjustment* opens to good reviews; Williams fights bouts of depression and nervousness.

1961

The Night of the Iguana opens in New York and wins New York Drama Critics Circle Award.

1962

Cuban missile crisis; Williams appears on the cover of *Time* and is called a master of American drama.

1963

President John F. Kennedy is assassinated; Williams's companion, Frank Merlo, dies; Williams falls into a deep depression and relies heavily on drugs and alcohol.

1964

U.S. soldiers are committed to the Vietnam War.

1968

Martin Luther King Jr. is assassinated.

1969

America lands a man on the moon; Williams converts to Catholicism; suffers a second nervous breakdown and is committed to the psychiatric ward of a St. Louis hospital.

1972

Small Craft Warnings receives favorable reviews, the first positive reception since *The Night of the Iguana.*

1974

President Richard Nixon resigns.

1975

The last Americans are evacuated from Vietnam; Williams publishes his revealing autobiography, *Memoirs.*

1977

Williams writes *Vieux Carré* and several subsequent plays that are clearly autobiographical; none are commercially successful; Williams continues to suffer periods of depression initiated by drugs and alcohol.

1980

Williams's mother, Miss Edwina, dies; Williams receives the Medal of Freedom from President Jimmy Carter.

1982

Vietnam Veterans Memorial is unveiled.

1983

Williams chokes to death on a bottle cap at the Elysee Hotel in New York.

FOR FURTHER RESEARCH

BIOGRAPHICAL WORKS AND LETTERS BY THE PLAYWRIGHT

Albert Devlin, ed., *Conversations with Tennessee Williams.* Jackson: University Press of Mississippi, 1986.

Richard Leavitt, ed., *The World of Tennessee Williams.* New York: G.P. Putnam's Sons, 1978.

Donald Spoto, *The Kindness of Strangers: The Life of Tennessee Williams.* Boston: Little, Brown, 1985.

Mike Steen, *A Look at Tennessee Williams.* New York: Hawthorn, 1969.

Dakin Williams and Shepherd Mead, *Tennessee Williams: An Intimate Biography.* New York: Arbor House, 1983.

Edwina Williams and L. Freeman, *Remember Me to Tom.* New York: Putnam, 1963.

Tennessee Williams, *Memoirs.* New York: Doubleday, 1975.

Donald Windham, ed., *Tennessee Williams' Letters to Donald Windham.* New York: Holt, Rinehart & Winston, 1977.

Audrey Wood and Max Wilk, *Represented by Audrey Wood.* Garden City, NY: Doubleday, 1981.

ABOUT *THE GLASS MENAGERIE* AND WILLIAMS' PLAYS

C.W.E. Bigsby, *A Critical Introduction to Twentieth-Century American Drama.* Vol. 2: *Williams/Miller/Albee.* Cambridge, England: Cambridge University Press, 1984.

Roger Boxill, *Tennessee Williams.* New York: St. Martin's Press, 1987.

Francis Donahue, *The Dramatic World of Tennessee Williams.* New York: Frederick Ungar, 1964.

Signi Falk, *Tennessee Williams.* Boston: Twayne, 1978.

Foster Hirsh, *A Portrait of the Artist: The Plays of Tennessee Williams*. Port Washington, NY: Kennikat Press, 1978.

Walter Kerr, *Pieces at Eight*. London: Max Reinhart, 1958.

R.B. Parker, ed., *The Glass Menagerie: A Collection of Critical Essays*. Englewood Cliffs, NJ: Prentice-Hall, 1983.

Gene Phillips, *The Films of Tennessee Williams*. London: Associated University Presses, 1980.

Ingrid Rogers, *Tennessee Williams: A Moralist's Answer to the Perils of Life*. Frankfurt: Peter Lang, 1976.

Jac Tharpe, ed., *Tennessee Williams: A Tribute*. Jackson: University Press of Mississippi, 1977.

HISTORICAL BACKGROUND

Gerald M. Berkowitz, *American Drama of the Twentieth Century*. London: Longman, 1992.

Gerald Bordman, *The Concise Oxford Companion to American Theatre*. New York: Oxford University Press, 1987.

Oscar G. Brockett, *History of the Theatre*. Boston: Allyn and Bacon, Inc., 1987.

Martin Lamm, *Modern Drama*. New York: Philosophical Library, 1953.

Frederick Lumley, *Trends in 20th Century Drama*. New York: Oxford University Press, 1960.

David W. Sievers, *Freud on Broadway: A History of Psychoanalysis and the American Drama*. New York: Hermitage House, 1955.

G.J. Watson, *Drama: An Introduction*. New York: St. Martin's Press, 1983.

Gerald Weales, *American Drama Since World War II*. New York: Harcourt, Brace & World, 1962.

G.B. Wilson, *Three Hundred Years of American Drama and Theatre*. Englewood Cliffs, NJ: Prentice-Hall, Inc., 1973.

WORKS BY TENNESSEE WILLIAMS

Tennessee Williams's works are available in a wide variety of anthologies and reissues; therefore, facts of publication are omitted from the following list. All works are plays unless otherwise noted. The dates given are the years in which the plays were written, not necessarily performed.

"Can a Good Wife Be a Good Sport?" (short story) (1927)

"The Vengeance of Nitocris" (short story) (1928)

Moony's Kid Don't Cry (1934)

Cairo! Shanghai! Bombay! (1935)

Candles to the Sun (1935)

Headlines (1936)

The Magic Tower (1936)

Fugitive Kind (1936)

Me, Vashya! (1937)

Spring Storm (1937)

Not About Nightingales (1939)

"The Field of Blue Children" (short story) (1939)

Battle of Angels (1939)

At Liberty (1939)

The Long Goodbye (1940)

The Purification (1940)

The Dark Room (1940)

The Case of the Crushed Petunias (1941)

I Rise in Flame, Cried the Phoenix (1941)

Auto Da Fé (1941)

The Frosted Glass Coffin (1941)

Hello from Bertha (1941)

This Property Is Condemned (1941)

The Lady of Larkspur Lotion (1941)

Stairs to the Roof (1942)

The Last of My Solid Gold Watches (1942)

You Touched Me! (1942)

The Glass Menagerie (1943)

27 Wagons Full of Cotton (1944)

Portrait of a Madonna (1944)

Lord Byron's Love Letter (1944)

The Strangest Kind of Romance (1944)

The Long Stay Cut Short (1945)

Summer and Smoke (1945)

Ten Blocks on the Camino Real (1946)

A Streetcar Named Desire (1947)

Steps Must Be Gentle (1947)

A Perfect Analysis Given by a Parrot (1948)

The Rose Tattoo (1950)

*Talk to Me Like the Rain and
Let Me Listen* (1950)

*The Roman Spring of Mrs.
Stone* (novel) (1950)

Eccentricities of a Nightingale
(1951)

Something Unspoken (1952)

Senso/The Wanton Countess
(screenplay) (1953)

Camino Real (1953)

*Three Players of a Summer
Game* (1954)

Hard Candy: A Book of Stories
(short stories) (1954)

Cat on a Hot Tin Roof (1955)

Sweet Bird of Youth (1956)

In the Winter Cities: Poems
(poems) (1956)

Baby Doll (screenplay) (1956)

Orpheus Descending (1957)

Suddenly Last Summer (1957)

Period of Adjustment (1957)

*The Milk Train Doesn't Stop
Here Anymore* (1959)

The Fugitive Kind
(screenplay) (1960)

The Night of the Iguana
(1961)

Slapstick Comedy (1965)

Kingdom of Earth (1966)

Confessional (1967)

The Two-Character Play
(1967)

*The Knightly Quest: A Novella
and Twelve Short Stories*
(1968)

In the Bar of a Tokyo Hotel
(1968)

Demolition Downtown (1970)

I Can't Imagine Tomorrow
(1971)

Out Cry (1971)

Small Craft Warnings (1972)

*Eight Mortal Ladies Possessed:
A Book of Stories* (short
stories) (1974)

Créve Coeur (1975)

*This Is the Peaceable Kingdom,
or Good Luck God* (1975)

Lifeboat Drill (1975)

*Now the Cats with Jeweled
Claws* (1975)

*Moise and the World of
Reason* (novel) (1975)

Memoirs (autobiography)
(1975)

The Red Devil Battery Sign
(1976)

This Is (An Entertainment)
(1976)

Vieux Carré (1976)

*Androgyne, Mon Amour:
Poems* (poems) (1977)

Tiger Tail (1978)

Where I Live: Selected Essays
(essays) (1978)

Clothes for a Summer Hotel
(1979)

*Will Mr. Merriweather Return
from Memphis?* (1979)

*Kirche, Küche, und Kinder: An
Outrage for the Stage* (1979)

A House Not Meant to Stand
(1980)

*Something Cloudy, Something
Clear* (1980)

The Bag People (1982)

*It Happened the Day the Sun
Rose, and Other Stories*
(short stories) (1982)

*Stopped Rocking and Other
Screenplays* (screenplays)
(published 1984)

Collected Stories (short
stories) (published 1985)

INDEX